ENDORSEMENTS

Christine's devotionals are a gift to the church worldwide! She has a rare gift of being able to hear from God through nature, encounters with friends, meeting strangers, and the rhythms of everyday life. Thus inspired, encouraged, or challenged, she engages with the Bible and opens wonderful insight for the reader! There is genuine joy and excitement as the Lord speaks to her and she passes on that new "illumination" to others through her devotionals. I passed copies of her books to members of my local church who have been richly blessed to travel this enlightening journey with Christine!

In her most recent devotional book, Christine will uplift, provoke, and minister to you as she focuses on God's compassion. I wholeheartedly recommend Christine and this book to you- prepare to be illuminated!

Rev. Nigel James
Former Tour Pastor to the Band, Third Day
Current Pastor of New Life Church, Barry, Wales, UK

A friend gave me a book entitled, *God's Presence Illuminated,* saying it would be perfect for my nursing home ministry. My first impression was that the author, Christine Fisher, had a beautiful and unique way of interpreting Scripture and incorporating God's words into everyday life.

A few weeks later, I had the honor of meeting Christine and immediately felt at ease in her presence. After listening to her speak, I sensed there was something special about this girl. Before parting company, she gave me her second book, *God's Love Illuminated.*

As a chaplain in a nursing home, I have a daily prayer session. We open with prayer and then I share the readings of the day. I have since incorporated Christine's books into my daily service, as they are a perfect fit. Each day has a Scripture reading, followed by her reflections on God's word, which gives a beautiful message for us to discuss.

Christine writes in such a caring, loving, and personal way. Her words have helped open my eyes to see and feel God's presence. One day, I observed a visiting husband holding his wife's hand. Unable to speak, she stared into his eyes. I knew, without a doubt, that I was witnessing true love—God's Love. Recently I read a daily passage to the group from Christine's book, *God's Presence Illuminated.* As the residents commented on her words in a beautiful encounter, I looked into their eyes and felt I was looking at Jesus.

Christine Fisher's words are truly an extension of God's love for all of us to experience each day. Her "holy" words come from her heart and each day lead me closer to our Lord. It is a true honor to know Christine and to call her my "little sister." I am excited about her new book, *God's Compassion Illuminated* and I look forward to sharing it with my nursing home family.

Deacon Mike
Peregrine Senior Living Chaplain

Other books by Christine M. Fisher:

God's Presence Illuminated: Treasured Thoughts to Inspire Hope and Light
God's Love Illuminated: Treasured Thoughts to Inspire Walking in God's Abundant Love

TREASURED THOUGHTS
TO INSPIRE FOLLOWING GOD'S WAY

GOD'S
COMPASSION
Illuminated

A 90-DAY DEVOTIONAL

May experiencing God's boundless compassion illuminated in your life continue to shine into the lives of others. Be inspired following God's way.

Psalm 103:8
Ephesians 4:32

♡ *Christine*

CHRISTINE M. FISHER

God's Compassion Illuminated
Treasured Thoughts to Inspire Following God's Way
Christine M. Fisher

To contact the author:
christine@hopetoinspireyou.com
www.hopetoinspireyou.com

Copyright 2022 © Christine M. Fisher. All rights reserved. Except for brief quotations for review purposes, no part of this book may be reproduced in any form without prior written permission from the author.

Published by:

Mary Ethel

Mary Ethel Eckard
Frisco, Texas

Library of Congress Catalog Number: 2022947779
ISBN (Print): 979-8-9868496-3-8
ISBN (E-book): 979-8-9868496-4-5

All Scripture quotations, unless otherwise indicated, are taken from the Holy Bible, New International Version ®, NIV ®, Copyright © 1973, 1978, 1984, 2011 by Biblica, Inc. Used by permission. All rights reserved worldwide. Scripture quotations marked ESV are taken from the ESV® Bible (Th e Holy Bible, English Standard Version®). ESV® Text Edition: 2016. Copyright © 2001 by Crossway, a publishing ministry of Good News Publishers. Th e ESV® text has been reproduced in cooperation with and by permission of Good News Publishers. Unauthorized reproduction of this publication is prohibited. Scripture quotations marked MSG are taken from THE MESSAGE, copyright © 1993, 2002, 2018 by Eugene H. Peterson. Used by permission of NavPress. All rights reserved. Represented by Tyndale House Publishers, Inc. Scripture quotations marked NLT are taken from the Holy Bible, New Living Translation, copyright © 1996, 2004, 2007, 2013, 2015 by Tyndale House Foundation. Used by permission of Tyndale House Publishers, Inc., Carol Stream, Illinois 60188. All rights reserved. Scripture quotations taken from the NASB® New American Standard Bible®, Copyright © 1960, 1971, 1977, 1995, 2020 by Th e Lockman Foundation. Used by permission. All rights reserved. www.lockman.org

CONTENTS

Dedication xi
Foreword xiii
Introduction xv

SECTION 1: GOD'S COMPASSION ILLUMINATED IN PEOPLE 1

   1. God Multiplies 3
   2. A Drink of Water 7
   3. Crashing Down 10
   4. God's Presence Revealed 12
   5. Orchestration Of Our Steps 17
   6. Living Kindness 20
   7. Find the Blessing 24
   8. Lessons From A Third Day Concert 26
   9. Shine Brightly 31
 10. Scars 34
 11. The Pilgrimage of Life 38
 12. The Blessing of Ministry 42
 13. Building Trust 45
 14. Unity In Prayer 48
 15. Paid In Full 52
 16. Connections 55
 17. Appreciation 60

18. Holy Encounters 65
19. The Blessed Caregivers 68
20. Rock Bottom... 70
21. Daily Connection.. 75
22. The Power Source 78

SECTION 2: GOD'S COMPASSION ILLUMINATED IN SCRIPTURE 83

23. Rainbows 85
24. The Storms 89
25. God – Our Provider 92
26. Jesus' Baptism 94
27. The Power of Thoughts... 98
28. Joy and Sorrow...101
29. The Vineyard 106
30. Be Still 110
31. Burdens 113
32. Places of Honor 115
33. Servant of All 119
34. Water Reflections 122
35. A Rocked World 125
36. Confess 130
37. Do Not Cling.. 133
38. Prepare the Way 136
39. Agony of Suffering 143
40. Tree of Love 146
41. Boast In Weakness 150
42. Living Like the End 153
43. Second Chances 158
44. Heart of Stone...161

SECTION 3: GOD'S COMPASSION ILLUMINATED IN ACTIVITIES 165

- 45. The Littlest Details 167
- 46. An Invitation 169
- 47. Divine Encounters 173
- 48. Airports 175
- 49. Brokenhearted 177
- 50. Day By Day 181
- 51. Patches of Godlight 186
- 52. Our Gifts 189
- 53. Perception 193
- 54. Mission Reflections 196
- 55. Waiting 200
- 56. Working Together in Harmony 202
- 57. The Radiance of God 205
- 58. Rainbow Reflections 208
- 59. God Day 212
- 60. Silence 215
- 61. Gratitude 218
- 62. Adventure of A Lifetime 222
- 63. A Time to Rest 225
- 64. God Incidents 228
- 65. Dance in the Rain 230
- 66. A Day of Blessings 234
- 67. Instruments of Love 237

SECTION 4: GOD'S COMPASSION ILLUMINATED IN THE HOLY LAND 241

- 68. The Fifth Gospel 243
- 69. Mount Arbel 248
- 70. Nazareth 252

71.	Bethlehem	254
72.	Shepherd's Field	256
73.	Jordan River	258
74.	Mount of Temptation	261
75.	Judean Desert	264
76.	Cana	267
77.	Capernaum	270
78.	Sea of Galilee	274
79.	Mount of Beatitudes	277
80.	Tabgha	282
81.	Magdala	284
82.	Bethsaida	288
83.	Dominus Flevit and Upper Room	290
84.	Garden of Gethsemane	294
85.	St Peter of Gallicantu	297
86.	Holy Sepulchre	303
87.	Church of the Resurrection	309
88.	Primacy of St Peter	312
89.	Old City of Jerusalem and Masada	317
90.	Dead Sea and Jaffa	322

Farewell to the Holy Land Pilgrimage	329
Conclusion	331
About the Author	335
Notes	337

DEDICATION

This book is written with gratitude to God for the gift of compassion He bestows upon our lives. It is a privilege to have that compassion flow through us into the lives of all we encounter.

With gratitude to Michael for allowing me the use of his lake house on Lake Ontario where I spent most of my time working on this manuscript. God's presence engulfed me with love, peace, and tranquility. The water and the glorious sunsets were the perfect combination to unite me with the Lord. What a treasured time of ministry and refreshment!

I remain grateful for the many people God has put in my life who have encouraged my writing ministry since September 2014, when I started writing for my website, www.hopetoinspireyou.com. God has been faithful in continuing weekly inspiration for eight years so far.

Thank you to all who, through the years, have encouraged and supported the sharing of my heart via the website, which has led to this third book. You have a special place deep in my heart and your presence in my life is a gift.

FOREWORD

I have known Christine since our children were little ones, attending pre-kindergarten. During those school years, we attended many school functions together. Christine was and is still often quiet and shy, but that is because she has this God-given ability to observe, take note, and put into action any need that needs to be met for anyone God places on her precious heart.

We became even closer friends when we learned we both treasure the band, Third Day. Over the years, we have attended many shows together, worshiping in song and celebrating as sisters in Christ. In addition to our music interests, we also share our love for the ocean and savor time spent at the beach. With my feet digging into the warm sand, I often attempt to pen my thoughts as I stare into the endless rolling waves. When I share my writings with Christine, she graciously replies with encouragement and love.

When asked if I would write this foreword, I was completely humbled, honored, and, truth be told, intimidated! What in the world could I write that could make you, the reader, comprehend how amazing and gifted Christine is? How can I put into words what this sweet soul means to me and how I have been blessed by her? This woman has been my prayer warrior (also known as my angel on earth) since the first day we met, and more so over the last couple of years as I have battled a thorn in my side. Whenever I seemed to be at my lowest point, Christine would send a loving and encouraging text, out of the blue, lifting me in prayer. Her writings have given me so much hope and a bright pathway through some very dark times. Her ability to see beauty in the simplicity of life and nature and then connect it to Scripture inspires me and makes me want to be a better human.

Christine was and still is there to walk alongside me. For the last year, she has graciously sent me a copy of her reflection every week. I eagerly await her email, not only for the inspiration it provides but also for the fact that she asks my opinion, which honors my heart.

Those of you who have read Christine's books or website reflections know how meaningful the heart shape is to her. Now, whenever I see anything heart-shaped, from mud puddles to potato chips, I immediately think of Christine. Her obedience to God's call, to write and share with us, keeps me yearning to be better, to love harder, and to see God in all things. Thank you, Christine, for letting me go on this journey with you and for letting us see God's goodness through your eyes and heart.

Laura Sage

INTRODUCTION

"Praise the Lord, my soul, and forget not all his benefits— who forgives all your sins and heals all your diseases, who redeems your life from the pit and crowns you with love and compassion, who satisfies your desires with good things so that your youth is renewed like the eagle's."
~ Psalm 103:2-5

As I was working on my second book, *God's Love Illuminated,* God continued to reveal His presence, not only through the hearts I found in rocks, mud, clouds, etc., but in rainbows. The beauty of a rainbow, with its array of colors, is fascinating to behold. I see rainbows as a sign of God's compassion, a natural extension of His love.

The biblical definition of compassion is: "A feeling of deep sympathy and sorrow for another who is hurting, in pain, or has misfortune, and is accompanied by a strong desire to help the suffering."

The strong desire to help the suffering means we need to put the feeling of compassion into action. True compassion changes the way we live. Our best example is to look at the lives of God the Father and Jesus, His only Son.

God demonstrates true compassion throughout the entire Bible. Because of His compassion, God devised a plan to save mankind as soon as Adam and Eve sinned by eating from the tree of knowledge. God's compassion saved Israel, saved the world and mankind from being destroyed by a flood, and sent a Savior, Jesus, to die on the cross for our salvation. Sending Jesus to walk this earth as a human showed God's compassion by giving us someone to whom we can relate in our humanness. Jesus was both divinity and humanity. Jesus' compassion shines forth in His willingness to follow God's way in obedience to be a sacrifice for us. He also showed compassion in the way He loved, healed, and befriended the worst of sinners.

May these devotions illuminate your way so you see God's compassion and mercy in the people you meet, Scripture stories, the activities you participate in, and walking in Jesus' footsteps in the Holy Land. As you take time to reflect on each story, may you be inspired to embrace God's abundant compassion in your faith journey. My prayer is that you will see God's compassion for you through a different lens and walk closer to Him. May the ending Scripture for each day reveal a facet of God's compassion and mercy for you personally.

God's compassion illuminated.

Section 1

GOD'S COMPASSION ILLUMINATED IN PEOPLE

"As a father has compassion on his children,
so the Lord has compassion on those who fear him;
for he knows how we are formed,
he remembers that we are dust."
~ Psalm 103:13-14

God formed man out of the dust of the earth and breathed His breath of life into him. We are descendants of the first man, Adam, formed in God's image and likeness. Therefore, we have many of the same attributes as God.

God is loving and compassionate toward all who call upon Him. We should strive daily to live in God's love and compassion and share that with all. May we lavishly share His compassion.

God's compassion illuminated in people.

"The purpose of life is not to be happy.
It is to be useful, to be honorable, to be compassionate,
to have it make some difference that you have lived and lived well."
~ Ralph Waldo Emerson

1

God Multiplies

Do you think the few dollars you put in the Salvation Army bucket won't help much?

Do you think the little food you have when unexpected company shows up won't be enough?

Do you think a simple act of sharing a smile can brighten someone's day?

God can use
>the smallest of things
>>in our lives and in this world
>>>to bring glory to His kingdom.

> *"While Jesus was in the Temple, he watched the rich people dropping their gifts in the collection box. Then a poor widow came by and dropped in two small coins. 'I tell you the truth,' Jesus said, 'this poor widow has given more than all the rest of them. For they have given a tiny part of their surplus, but she, poor as she is, has given everything she has.'"*
> ~ Luke 21:1-4 (NLT)

The rich people were only willing to share a small part of the extra they had. They were not willing to give their all to God with sincere hearts. Jesus teaches us the value of a poor widow giving two small coins, which were worth very little monetarily.

The widow…

>had a sincere heart that wanted to honor God in her giving.
>gave everything she had, showing her trust and faith in God.

When we
> share from the heart,
>> God multiplies.

> *"Jesus saw the huge crowd as he stepped from the boat, and he had compassion on them and healed their sick. That evening the disciples came to him and said, 'This is a remote place, and it's already getting late. Send the crowds away so they can go to the villages and buy food for themselves.' But Jesus said, 'That isn't necessary— you feed them.' 'But we have only five loaves of bread and two fish!' they answered. 'Bring them here,' he said. Then he told the people to sit down on the grass. Jesus took the five loaves and two fish, looked up toward heaven, and blessed them. Then, breaking the loaves into pieces, he gave the bread to the disciples, who distributed it to the people. They all ate as much as they wanted, and afterward, the disciples picked up twelve baskets of leftovers. About 5,000 men were fed that day, in addition to all the women and children!"*
> ~ Matthew 14:14-21 (NLT)

In this passage, we see the heart of Jesus filled with compassion and love. Jesus' compassion extended to the crowd's physical ailments as well as their need for food. The disciples wanted to dismiss the crowd, reasoning that the people could go buy their own food. They did not see a way to feed more than 5,000 men with only five loaves of bread and two fish.

Jesus was able to invoke God's spirit to bless the little food they had. God provided enough food for the multitude of people and had twelve baskets of leftovers.

When we
> give the little we have,
>> God multiplies.

> *"Here is another illustration Jesus used: 'The Kingdom of Heaven is like a mustard seed planted in a field. It is the smallest of all seeds, but it becomes the largest of garden plants; it grows into a tree, and birds come and make nests in its branches.'"*
> ~ Matthew 13:31-32 (NLT)

In Jesus' day, the mustard seed was the smallest seed used by farmers and gardeners. With the most favorable conditions, the tree could reach ten feet in height, providing great shade for refuge. This illustration shows us how the Kingdom of Heaven, starting small, can spread throughout the whole world. It is a place of rest. God's power yields a rich crop.

When we
>> sow the smallest of seeds,
>>> God multiplies.

May we be encouraged to…

>> see ways we can give to others with a sincere heart.
>> share what we have in trust and faith, knowing God will provide.
>> give sacrificially.
>> find ways to extend Jesus' compassion and love.
>> see how God uses the little we have, even if just a smile.
>> offer our lives to the Lord daily.
>> sow the smallest of seeds, like complimenting someone or holding a door open.
>> see how the smallest of seeds we sow grow into great goodness.
>> see how God uses the smallest of things to transform His kingdom.

Remember when we…

>> share from the heart,
>>> God multiplies.

    give the little we have,
        God multiplies.
    sow the smallest of seeds,
        God multiplies.

God can use
    the smallest of things
        in our lives and in this world
            to bring glory to His kingdom.

REFLECTION:

What little thing did you offer to the Lord that He multiplied?
How did God provide a little in your life that went a long way?

"I have compassion for these people;
they have already been with me three days and have nothing to eat."
        ~ Mark 8:2

2

A Drink of Water

I am in awe of God's perfect timing of events in our lives, and I want to shout it from the rooftops. As I was finishing a walk in my neighborhood, I noticed two young girls trying to get the attention of a neighbor who was mowing his lawn. They were excited, jumping up and down, saying politely, "Sir, would you like a drink?" though he was unaware.

I could see the girls had a drink stand. My first thought was that I should take another route to avoid them as I did not have money with me. I opted to walk by them. They were still jumping up and down with excitement, and said, "Would you like some water?" I said, "I don't have money with me." The older girl said, "That's okay. It is free." I figured it would make them happy to accept it, so I said, "Yes."

They had big red plastic cups ready, and a lovely big blue glass pitcher filled with water. The two girls worked together to give me my drink and asked me if it was enough. They also inquired if I wanted them to take my cup when I was finished, as they had a place for them. Trying to make conversation with them, I asked if they had other customers. They said I was the first person they served. As I was drinking, I noticed the younger girl holding a sign. I don't recall exactly what it said, but at the end, I saw $1.

As I walked away,
>I thought how kind that,
>>even though they wanted money for the drink,
>>>they freely provided refreshment to me
>>>>even though I didn't have money on me.

As I proceeded home, I was inspired to pay the girls because of their kindness and generosity; to maybe be Jesus to them without using words.

I walked home, found ten dimes so they could easily share the money equally, and headed back to their stand. As I approached, another lady was walking her dog who took water despite not having money either. The girls remembered me, and I handed them the money, simply saying I wanted to pay them.

> *"When a Samaritan woman came to draw water, Jesus said to her, 'Will you give me a drink?'(His disciples had gone into the town to buy food.) The Samaritan woman said to him, 'You are a Jew and I am a Samaritan woman. How can you ask me for a drink?' (For Jews do not associate with Samaritans.) Jesus answered her, 'If you knew the gift of God and who it is that asks you for a drink, you would have asked him and he would have given you living water.' 'Sir,' the woman said, 'you have nothing to draw with and the well is deep. Where can you get this living water? Are you greater than our father Jacob, who gave us the well and drank from it himself, as did also his sons and his livestock?' Jesus answered, 'Everyone who drinks this water will be thirsty again, but whoever drinks the water I give them will never thirst. Indeed, the water I give them will become in them a spring of water welling up to eternal life.' The woman said to him, 'Sir, give me this water so that I won't get thirsty and have to keep coming here to draw water.'"*
> ~ John 4:7-15

I thought of the parallels between the two girls I encountered and this Bible story.

These girls freely gave me water just as
      Jesus freely gave this woman water; a gift,
           just as He gives to all of us who seek Him.

Hopefully, giving the girls money for their water, to share my joy, brought them joy just like…

> the woman shared her joy to help others come to know Jesus as the Messiah.

You never know when you will be blessed:
> a simple drink of water on my walk reminded me of Jesus,
>> the Living Water, who is always at work and present in our lives.

REFLECTION:

In what way have you provided "water" for someone?
How has God refreshed you through another person?

> *"Is anyone thirsty?*
> *Come and drink— even if you have no money!*
> *Come, take your choice of wine or milk—*
> *it's all free!"*
> ~ Isaiah 55:1 (NLT)

3

Crashing Down

Have you ever been in a situation where it seemed you were on top of the world and everything seemed too good to be true? What happened next? Did your world seem to suddenly come crashing down?

Sometimes it seems unfair, and you don't know how you are going to deal with the issue at hand.

I felt like that when I was diagnosed with Stage 0 DCIS (Ductal Carcinoma In Situ) Breast Cancer. It is the best stage and form to have, but at the same time, life changed in an instant. The Breast Center still treated it as "cancer," and even sent me brochures on support groups. To this day, I struggle with saying, "I had cancer." It seems that something that is Stage 0 should be insignificant.

There were a few months of torture, first waiting for tests to determine the diagnosis, then researching options and talking with others who had a similar issue. That was followed by trying to decide which treatments to pursue, seeing specialists, having one surgery, then finding out I needed a second one a week later and waiting for the results. The hardest part was discerning God's leading to go against the protocol of radiation, which didn't feel like the right choice for me. I am thankful I have not had any reoccurrences in the last nine years. I endured so little compared to many others. To this day, I wonder why the Lord would spare me while so many others endure much suffering.

I have seen friends who have lost loved ones, had a miscarriage or walked through hardship with their children. Our world crashing down could be something as discouraging as losing a friendship over a misunderstanding. When my world comes crashing down, my faith gets shaken, even though I like to think it is strong. Sometimes it is hard to remain steadfast.

What can we do to stay strong in our faith? We can …

> Surround ourselves with faithful people who encourage and lift us.
> Listen to encouraging Christian music to inspire us.
> Ask other Christians to pray for us.
> Read the Bible and other encouraging Christian books.
> Look for God's blessings, even the smallest ones.
> Remind ourselves that God is still in control and leading us.

When we experience these tough times, it is important to reach out to God and others. Just as important is trying to be aware when others need our compassion, listening ear, or encouragement to help them through a difficult time. Are we there for them when they need a touch of kindness?

REFLECTION:

When did your world come crashing down?
How did you experience God's love and presence through it?

> *"Let your compassion come to me that I may live,*
> *for your law is my delight."*
> ~ Psalm 119:77

4

God's Presence Revealed

I am enjoying spirit-filled conversations with new friends while sharing my books. My life is enriched by these warm exchanges which often spark reflections of some sort.

In the second face-to-face conversation, a friend was curious to hear my story of how God led me to my writing ministry. As I shared, he was reminded of something a college chaplain shared, encouraging students to see God's presence revealed in their lives:

> "Pay attention…
> Be astonished…
> Tell about it…"

While celebrating the birth of Jesus one year, it occurred to me that the shepherds and Magi are perfect examples of these three things.

> *"That night there were shepherds staying in the fields nearby, guarding their flocks of sheep. Suddenly, an angel of the Lord appeared among them, and the radiance of the Lord's glory surrounded them. They were terrified, but the angel reassured them. 'Don't be afraid!' he said. 'I bring you good news that will bring great joy to all people. The Savior— yes, the Messiah, the Lord— has been born today in Bethlehem, the city of David! And you will recognize him by this sign: You will find a baby wrapped snugly in strips of cloth, lying in a manger.'"*
> ~ Luke 2:8-12 (NLT)

"When the angels had returned to heaven, the shepherds said to each other, 'Let's go to Bethlehem! Let's see this thing that has happened, which the Lord has told us about.' They hurried to the village and found Mary and Joseph. And there was the baby, lying in the manger. After seeing him, the shepherds told everyone what had happened and what the angel had said to them about this child. All who heard the shepherds' story were astonished, but Mary kept all these things in her heart and thought about them often."
~ Luke 2:15-19 (NLT)

The shepherds, just simple ordinary people, were the people to whom God chose to announce the good news. Aren't we just like those shepherds, being simple ordinary people? Shouldn't we, too, announce the good news?

Notice how the shepherds:

> Paid attention…
>
>> to the angel of the Lord, who had the radiance of the Lord's glory surround the shepherds. I imagine their ears perked up, too, with hearing "*…good news that will bring great joy…*"
>
> Were astonished…
>
>> so much so that they wanted to go see the Messiah right away. The shepherds left everything and hurried to Bethlehem.
>
> Told about it…
>
>> after seeing the baby Jesus, *"the shepherds told everyone what had happened."* With their lives forever changed and so full of joy, they couldn't help but share. Isn't it

interesting to note that *"all who heard the shepherds' story were astonished"* too?

"After Jesus was born in Bethlehem in Judea, during the time of King Herod, Magi from the east came to Jerusalem and asked, 'Where is the one who has been born king of the Jews? We saw his star when it rose and have come to worship him.'"
~ Matthew 2:1-2

"Then Herod called the Magi secretly and found out from them the exact time the star had appeared. He sent them to Bethlehem and said, 'Go and search carefully for the child. As soon as you find him, report to me, so that I too may go and worship him.' After they had heard the king, they went on their way, and the star they had seen when it rose went ahead of them until it stopped over the place where the child was. When they saw the star, they were overjoyed. On coming to the house, they saw the child with his mother Mary, and they bowed down and worshiped him. Then they opened their treasures and presented him with gifts of gold, frankincense and myrrh."
~ Matthew 2:7-11

Notice how the Magi:

> Paid attention…

>> as they were diligent in looking up at the sky. The Magi, most likely astrologers, were attentive to noticing a special star that suddenly appeared in the sky.

> Were astonished…

>> at seeing such a unique star. The Magi knew, without a doubt, that they had never seen such a star before. Even though Herod technically sent the Magi to follow the star,

they were curious to see what they would find. I believe they were astonished at seeing the star lead their way and stop at the exact spot where the child Jesus was. As Scripture says, they were *"overjoyed."* The Magi brought special gifts, as they knew this was no ordinary star that led them to the king of the Jews.

Told about it...

after following the star and seeing the king of the Jews. We know the Magi were Gentiles, people who were not Jewish. They were originally not part of the chosen people. However, bringing gifts to the Christ child demonstrates that they recognized Him as the king of the Jews, whom they then worshiped. I have to believe they shared this good news with all they met after their encounter.

Isn't it encouraging to know God reveals Himself to everyone?
He is impartial.

May God reveal His presence in your everyday life. As each new day unfolds, be encouraged to:

Pay attention...

to the still, small voice you hear.
to the beauty of nature all around you.
to the people God places in your path.

Be astonished...

at the ways God uses your life to encourage others.
at the ways God sends others to minister to you in your time of need.

at the simple joys in life.

Tell about it…

    by sharing God in your life with others.
    via whatever gifts God has given to you.
    by writing a love letter to God or journaling.

REFLECTION:

When was God's presence revealed powerfully in your life? Were you astonished and told others about it?

> *"Let the whole earth sing to the Lord!*
> *Each day proclaim the good news that he saves.*
> *Publish his glorious deeds among the nations.*
> *Tell everyone about the amazing things he does."*
>   ~ 1 Chronicles 16:23-24 (NLT)

5

Orchestration Of Our Steps

God is always full of surprises ...
   God is always revealing His presence...
      God is always orchestrating our footsteps.

Another sunny Sunday was forecast, so it was a perfect fall day for a road trip to a park. As my husband and I pulled up to the local sub shop, we noticed an older woman pushing a wired cart. She was struggling a bit as she entered the restaurant and sat down. Seeing her, I felt an inkling and told my husband, "I think we should buy her some food." My husband went in to pick up our order and asked the woman if she wanted some food. She said, "Yes," so he ordered what she wanted and gave it to her. I share that story because it proves how God is always orchestrating our footsteps and the events in our lives.

> *"We can make our plans, but the Lord determines our steps."*
> ~ Proverbs 16:9 (NLT)

When we arrived at the park, it was sprinkling, a little foggy, and cloudy, though the forecast called for no rain. As we walked, I noticed a couple near the lake. The gentleman was brave enough to go swimming while the lady returned to the parking lot. She was hoping she was in the right place for the water baptisms that were going to take place. We had a lovely conversation as she waited for the rest of the group to arrive.

I had the unexpected pleasure of watching the lady's husband, along with two teenage girls, get baptized in this lake. It was wonderful to hear each of them make a public proclamation of accepting Jesus as their Lord and

Savior, taking the next step in their faith journey. Amazingly, the pastor had a stroke two weeks earlier and had just been released from the hospital. He braved the water despite a few side effects he was still experiencing.

These events caused me to reflect on Jesus' baptism in the Jordan River by John the Baptist,

> *"And behold, a voice from heaven said,*
> *'This is my beloved Son, with whom I am well pleased.'"*
> ~ Matthew 3:17 (ESV)

I am sure God was saying this same phrase, *"This is my beloved son (daughter), with whom I am well pleased,"* as these three people were baptized. What rejoicing there was in heaven.

Seeing the two teens took my thoughts back to the previous night when I was attending my church service. It was God's perfect timing to ride the elevator with a teen boy who assists in lighting the candles and making sure everything is set up in church. As we got into the elevator, I said, "Thank you for all you do for the church and church family. It is so nice to see young people love the Lord and be involved." Earlier this year, this teen brought a friend to the Lord, and I witnessed his baptism. I told him how special that was, too, as we conversed.

> *"The Lord directs the steps of the godly.*
> *He delights in every detail of their lives."*
> ~ Psalm 37:23 (NLT)

The day was blessed with special God moments by being obedient to His voice and taking time to converse with strangers. It was a perfect blend of realizing how important people are in our lives, sharing faith stories, having quiet time with the Lord, and observing His beautiful creation.

Only God can orchestrate the special events of our days and the blessing of each moment.

May we see God revealing His presence, orchestrating our footsteps each day.

REFLECTION:

How have you witnessed God's presence today?
What special orchestration did God provide?

"Put on then, as God's chosen ones, holy and beloved, compassionate hearts, kindness, humility, meekness, and patience."
~ Colossians 3:12 (ESV)

6

Living Kindness

Reading a book entitled *Praying for Strangers* and hearing a talk entitled, "Live a Life of Kindness" provided inspiration. Each of us can make this world a better place for at least one person every day by living a life of kindness and sharing the light of Christ within us.

The speaker said,
> "You will never look into the eyes of someone God does not love. Always be kind."

If we look at life from that perspective, does it change the way we live, treat, and even view the people we see? What if, while shopping, walking around the neighborhood, working, exercising at the gym, or attending a gathering, we consider how special each person is to God? God's love is the same for everyone. Isn't that a perfect reason to be kind?

Do you live a life of kindness?

Living a life of kindness has more to do with our attitude, the attitude of our hearts and soul, and then taking action. Living a life of kindness is having a heart open to the Lord with a focus on sharing the Christ in us, as we go about the ordinary of life.

The online Cambridge dictionary defines kindness as: "The quality of being generous, helpful, and caring about other people, or an act showing this quality."

"No act of kindness, no matter how small is ever wasted."
~ Aesop

I highly recommend the book, *Praying for Strangers.* One year the author, River Jordan, decided to start praying for a stranger each day as the Lord prompted. Though an introvert and a writer, she would daily step out of her comfort zone, following the Lord's prompting, to share kindness by caring and praying for another.

A simple extending, "I will be praying for you today," often results in a two-minute exchange of her learning a little of someone's story. It lets people know they are valued and cared for. This became a reality in my life after finishing the book. I was at a retreat where I did not know anyone. A lady I was standing next to mentioned how she liked the shirt I was wearing that said, "Yes, there is always hope." I learned that her daughter committed suicide a few years earlier. I asked her name and told her I would be praying for her and her family, and she said the same for me. I took her as the first "stranger" I was praying for. We never know what others are going through or what their lives have been like. We can shower their lives with kindness because they know we care.

The talk was given by a man named Chet, who is better known as the "Bread Man." He is a retired educator who, for almost 20 years, has baked over 96,000 loaves of bread. He is living a life of kindness through the act of baking bread and freely distributing it to those he encounters.

Why does Chet do this?
> "I've learned that the bread is good, but the feeling of kindness is what captures the hearts and minds of the people I meet."

It was enlightening to listen to his story and to see how a loaf of bread, coupled with kindness, can bless lives.

Other benefits of Chet's bread ministry are that…

> he is community for others– being part of something bigger than himself.
> it lets others know they are important.
> it changes the world, one person and one loaf of bread at a time.
> he finds goodness in everyone.
> he cultivates an attitude of gratitude in his own life.
> it shows how kindness can change one's perspective.
> it enables him to share love, the most important ingredient in the bread.

Chet, too, often learns about someone's story. Learning a little of their story, showing kindness, and caring reminds me of what Jesus did when He walked this earth.

Feel free to take a few moments and read the Bible verses below relating to the stories as noted.

> Think about the adulteress woman the Pharisees brought to Jesus. (John 8:1-11)
> Jesus went to dinner at Zacchaeus' house, the chief tax collector who cheated people. (Luke 19:1-10)
> Jesus touched a leper and healed him. (Luke 5:12-14)

Even knowing each of their stories, Jesus showed kindness. He gave us examples of how the power of kindness can change lives, creating community where brokenness can be healed, resulting in wholeness, love, and joy.

Live a life of kindness~
> Be kind to unkind people; they need kindness the most.

"If you see someone falling behind, walk beside them.
If you see someone being ignored, find a way to include them.
If someone has been knocked down, lift them up.
Always remind people of their worth.
One small act could mean the world to them."
~ tinybuddha.com

Be the world of kindness
    one act at a time
        affirming others' value as well as your own.

"You will never look into the eyes of someone
God does not love. Always be kind."

REFLECTION:

When did someone extend an act of kindness, caring about your story? Who did God put in your path that shared their story with you?

"Be kind and compassionate to one another,
forgiving each other, just as in Christ God forgave you."
~ Ephesians 4:32

7

Find the Blessing

This reflection is a result of listening to a friend as she and I tried to understand and process her experience.

Have you ever been in a situation when you needed to share a burden or a personal prayer request with someone?

Did you feel like you were at a breaking point, being overwhelmed by dealing with heartbreaking circumstances?

Maybe you thought of some longtime friends or people you were there to support during their time of trial and when you were brave enough to share, they did not give you support. They did not even say, "I'm sorry." They just changed the subject and shared their issues.

A simple heartfelt "I'm sorry" can make a world of difference. A lack of response can hurt us deeply and potentially even scar us from sharing with others. We may be left wondering about the point of the friendship.

My friend was feeling down about the reactions from the people she shared with and, as we were lamenting, she finally concluded it was time to release the hurt. She decided to dwell on the positives of the encounter she would soon be facing and to find the blessing there.

We don't need to have the answers.
    We just need to listen.
        "Lay on the ears" for others!

My prayer is that we may be encouraged to…

> be sensitive to someone who might need a caring spirit.
> think about our willingness to listen to or pray with someone who is reaching out.
> try to offer encouragement to people who are struggling.
> forgive those who have failed or hurt us.
> think of others' needs before our own.

May we be encouraged to…

> always look for the bright side, even in the worst of situations.
> look for the blessing God is providing, even if it is the smallest thing.
> find something positive, even when others let us down.
> continue to reach out to others in encouragement or prayer.

REFLECTION:

Who can you count on to listen with their heart when you are troubled? Who can count on you to share their burden with?

> *"You must be compassionate, just as your Father is compassionate."*
> ~ Luke 6:36 (NLT)

8

Lessons From A Third Day Concert

I have been a huge fan of Third Day, a Christian band, since first hearing them at a conference in September 2013. The messages in their songs speak to my soul, encourage, and uplift me. Going on several road trips with a friend to see Third Day helped me reflect on lessons I've learned through our travels.

It can be a real blessing to get away for a day from the routine of life.

> Most of our trips are over 24 hours due to the fact we have children, husbands, and responsibilities at home. The car rides give us a chance to catch up on life and have more in-depth conversations about faith. Though short on time, we come back refreshed and inspired.
>
> *"Therefore, we do not lose heart.*
> *Though outwardly we are wasting away,*
> *yet inwardly we are being renewed day by day."*
> *~ 2 Corinthians 4:16*

We need to trust the Lord in our travels.

> We have weathered the various elements on our travels. One time, the sun was shining as we left. It wasn't far into the trip when storm clouds began forming. Snow flurries started, followed by

more sun, snow showers, and eventually a period of snow causing low visibility. We were going 35-40 mph on the highway. We had no choice but to continue, slow and steady, even though it was difficult. Each time the conditions got bad, we had no idea how long it would last. It comforted me to know we had people at home praying for our safe travels. It was nice to have someone to share the adventure with. Together is better.

> *"When I am afraid, I will trust in you."*
> ~ Psalm 56:3

MEETING "STARS" CAN BE INTIMIDATING, BUT THEY ARE HUMANS JUST LIKE YOU AND ME. WE ARE REALLY ALL THE SAME.

I have been blessed to be part of the VIP experience with the four main guys from Third Day. Each time, I get nervous and probably appear scatterbrained. I need to remember they are people just like you and me. The guys are so down-to-earth that they make you feel comfortable. It is easy to put them on a pedestal, but they don't look at it that way. Their lives reflect how God created us all equal, though we have different talents or gifts.

> *"Then Peter began to speak: 'I now realize how true it is that God does not show favoritism but accepts from every nation the one who fears him and does what is right.'"*
> ~ Acts 10:34-35

IT IS A BLESSING TO MEET THE PEOPLE BEHIND THE SCENES TOO.

I had the honor of having my picture taken with the road pastor for Third Day, Nigel (who wrote an endorsement for this book). Through social media, I have gleaned from his wisdom when he posts parts of the devotionals he shares with the guys. Nigel is a humble man of God. It is so special the band has him to tour with them.

> *"...All of you, clothe yourselves with humility toward one another, because, 'God opposes the proud but shows favor to the humble.' Humble yourselves, therefore, under God's mighty hand, that he may lift you up in due time."*
> *~ 1 Peter 5:5-6*

IT IS A BLESSING TO MAKE OTHERS FEEL SPECIAL.

The guys of Third Day make their fans feel special and important. They take time to meet their fans and sign autographs. Doing this day after day must get tiring, but the guys never give that impression. They introduce themselves, shake hands, ask questions, and even thank their fans for coming. They, too, are humble men of God.

At one of our early concerts, Mac Powell, the lead singer, put his hand out to shake mine and said, "I know you from Twitter." That surprised me. From the many fans he has, he recognized little ole me. Since that time, we have been on a first-name basis, and we usually get a photo together.

> *"Do nothing out of selfish ambition or vain conceit. Rather, in humility value others above yourselves, not looking to your own interests but each of you to the interests of the others."*
> *~ Philippians 2:3-4*

IT IS IMPORTANT TO LET OTHERS KNOW HOW MUCH YOU ARE BLESSED BY THEM.

As a fan whose life has been touched by Third Day's music, I want to convey how blessed my life has been through their music. The first time I met them I had the idea to share a verse book I wrote years ago. It was fun to write each of them a personal message. I try to convey to them with my words, whether in person or via social media, how much they and their music bless my life.

> *"...It is more blessed to give than to receive."*
> ~ Acts 20:35

THIRD DAY CONCERTS ARE GREAT TIMES OF WORSHIP.

Having front row seats or being close to the front certainly adds to the specialness of the concerts. I close my eyes and immediately get lost in the lyrics of the songs as I worship the Lord.

> *"Come, let us sing for joy to the Lord; let us shout*
> *aloud to the Rock of our salvation.*
> *Let us come before him with thanksgiving and*
> *extol him with music and song."*
> ~ Psalm 95:1-2

GETTING OUT OF OUR COMFORT ZONE AND SHARING OUR FAITH WITH OTHER FANS IS A BLESSING.

My life has also been enriched through meeting more longtime fans of Third Day, called Gomers. I went to one concert to meet a Gomer I was friends with on social media but never met in person. We had been conversing and inspired each other to attend. It was a great blessing to meet her in person, along with a few other Gomers. Doing something out of my comfort zone, like talking with these strangers over a late-night dinner, was a blast. When we reach out to others and support one another, we are certainly blessed in unexpected ways.

"For where two or three gather in my name, there am I with them."
~ Matthew 18:20

I am truly thankful for the many ways I have been enriched since seeing Third Day for the first time.

It has had a ripple effect on my life...

> being inspired by Third Day's music.
> meeting Third Day in person.
> expanding my horizons to more social media.
> meeting many wonderful people through social media.
> inspiration to write again and share what is in my heart.
> joining a Christian blogger group to spread joy.
> meeting and reading inspiring posts.

REFLECTION:

Who has made you feel special and valued?
How have you shown others they are appreciated?

So, to the guys of Third Day (Nigel included!), I end with this...

"I thank my God every time I remember you. In all my prayers for all of you, I always pray with joy because of your partnership in the gospel from the first day until now, being confident of this, that he who began a good work in you will carry it on to completion until the day of Christ Jesus."
~ Philippians 1:3-6

9

Shine Brightly

I read something that inspired these thoughts.

Consider an old-fashioned flashlight that uses batteries. What do we do with a flashlight that starts to grow dim or stops working? Do we just throw it away?

> No, we put in fresh batteries.

What do we do when someone messes up in life and is in a dark space, not shining their light?

> We come alongside and help them.

What if the person's light still doesn't shine?

> We keep shining our light and sit with them patiently, sharing God's love.

What if we view our life as a flashlight? Is your life a bright, shining light?

> If it is, I bet God's Word is leading your life. You are probably enjoying a vibrant prayer life and experiencing a sense of community with like-minded friends as well.

Is our light becoming a bit dim?

> Do we need a change in routine to get our light shining brighter?
> Do we need someone to walk with us who will encourage us and help us find ways to shine our light brighter?
> Do we need some fresh batteries?
> Do we need to reach out to others for help to recharge our batteries?
> Do we need to cry out to God to share our hearts?

Sometimes we need new batteries so we can shine brightly once again.

What if we view our life as a battery?

How can we help one another shine? What kind of battery power can you provide for someone else?
- AA battery – offering affirmation, attentiveness
- AAA battery – offering affection, assurance, advice
- C battery – offering Christ's compassion
- D battery – offering direction

We can be encouraged to be both the flashlight and the battery…

> Let the flashlight of our lives shine bright and strong.
> Seek out people and ways to help our light shine brightly.
> Think of ways we can be a battery or battery charger for others.
> May our battery power be used to help others.

May our flashlight always shine for the Lord…

> We should not shine our flashlight so others can see us: we should shine so that, through our flashlight, others can see the Light of Christ.
> We can remember, too, that even if our light is not shining brightly, God never gives up on us.

REFLECTION:

Which battery power best describes how you shine for others?
Is your flashlight shining brightly?

> *"You are the light of the world. A town built on a hill cannot be hidden. Neither do people light a lamp and put it under a bowl. Instead they put it on its stand, and it gives light to everyone in the*

house. In the same way, let your light shine before others, that they may see your good deeds and glorify your Father in heaven."
~ Matthew 5:14-16

10

Scars

We all have scars of some type. When I say the word scars, what comes to mind?

    A physical scar you can see?

    An emotional scar you cannot see?

Do you have a physical scar?

    Does seeing it make you think about the event that caused the scar?

        Were you doing something you knew you shouldn't have?

        Was it just a silly incident?

            Was it self-inflicted or from someone else?

I have a physical scar under my chin. It happened on Labor Day when I was ten years old and swimming at my aunt's in-ground pool. My chin hit the side ledge of the pool as I jumped in. I should have gotten a stitch or two at the time, but we opted not to go to the hospital.

Are you aware of any emotional scars you have?

    Are they the result of a traumatic experience you have never shared?

Emotional or mental scars are not visible yet have a greater impact on our lives. Maybe you were abused, either physically or emotionally, bullied as a youngster, or neglected. These emotional scars can affect the way we view the world and others.

Have you thought about the scars Jesus endured in His humanity while on this earth? Jesus, too, experienced physical and emotional scars.

> "On the evening of that first day of the week, when the disciples were together, with the doors locked for fear of the Jewish leaders, Jesus came and stood among them and said, 'Peace be with you!' After he said this, he showed them his hands and side. The disciples were overjoyed when they saw the Lord. Again, Jesus said, 'Peace be with you! As the Father has sent me, I am sending you.' And with that he breathed on them and said, 'Receive the Holy Spirit. If you forgive anyone's sins, their sins are forgiven; if you do not forgive them, they are not forgiven.'
>
> "Now Thomas (also known as Didymus), one of the Twelve, was not with the disciples when Jesus came. So the other disciples told him, 'We have seen the Lord!' But he said to them, 'Unless I see the nail marks in his hands and put my finger where the nails were, and put my hand into his side, I will not believe.' A week later his disciples were in the house again, and Thomas was with them. Though the doors were locked, Jesus came and stood among them and said, 'Peace be with you!' Then he said to Thomas, 'Put your finger here; see my hands. Reach out your hand and put it into my side. Stop doubting and believe.' Thomas said to him, 'My Lord and my God!' Then Jesus told him, 'Because you have seen me, you have believed; blessed are those who have not seen and yet have believed.'"
> ~ John 20:19-29

This passage is after Jesus' resurrection and before His ascension into heaven. How interesting to note that in both appearances, Jesus first says, *"Peace be with you!"* The second thing He shows them are the physical scars, which are apparent from the nail marks on His hands and side. The disciples recognize Him from these visible scars on His body.

> "While they were still talking about this, Jesus himself stood among them and said to them, 'Peace be with you.' They were startled and frightened, thinking they saw a ghost. He said to them, 'Why are you troubled, and why do doubts rise in your minds? Look at my hands and my feet. It is I myself! Touch me and see; a ghost does not have flesh and bones, as you

see I have.' When he had said this, he showed them his hands and feet. And while they still did not believe it because of joy and amazement, he asked them, 'Do you have anything here to eat?' They gave him a piece of broiled fish, and he took it and ate it in their presence."
~ Luke 24:36-43

Luke's version of the same story also emphasizes the "peace" Jesus extends to the disciples. Here they believe they see a ghost, but Jesus' scars on His hands and feet prove who is standing in their midst. When eating with the disciples, Jesus, in His resurrected state, is also recognized.

"Then some began to spit at him; they blindfolded him, struck him with their fists, and said, 'Prophesy!' And the guards took him and beat him."
~ Mark 14:65

"For God made Christ, who never sinned, to be the offering for our sin, so that we could be made right with God through Christ."
~ 2 Corinthians 5:21 (NLT)

Imagine the emotional scars Jesus endured for you. He was spit upon, mocked, bullied, and made to carry a heavy cross on the way to Calvary. Jesus, an innocent man who did no wrong, was punished for your transgressions.

"From now on, don't let anyone trouble me with these things. For I bear on my body the scars that show I belong to Jesus."
~ Galatians 6:17 (NLT)

Paul, in this passage, relates how some physical scars on his body are most likely the result of standing for his belief in Jesus. Sometimes Christians, especially back in Jesus' day, endured great physical persecution for the sake of spreading the gospel message.

Jesus' scars, both His physical and emotional ones, are evidence of…

> the salvation and freedom we have in Christ.
> the reality of His presence in our lives.
> God's great love for us.

Because of Jesus' scars on His hands, feet, and side, can you too…

> be filled with peace?
> say, "My Lord and my God?"
> be sent in Jesus' name, willing to endure persecution?

The physical and emotional scars you possess are a natural part of life and serve a purpose. May God be glorified through the scars your life bears just as Jesus' scars did.

REFLECTION:

Can you surrender your emotional scars to the Lord?
Does knowing Jesus endured emotional trauma for you bring you closer to Him?

> *"But he was pierced for our transgressions, he was crushed for our iniquities; the punishment that brought us peace was on him, and by his wounds we are healed."*
> ~ Isaiah 53:5

11

The Pilgrimage of Life

I was inspired to watch a movie entitled *The Way* after hearing a sermon. In this movie, a father unexpectedly finds himself walking the Camino de Santiago, which is a roughly 500-mile trek. He meets a few people along the way, and they start traveling together. The father is challenged on his journey and is changed by the end of it.

There are many great takeaways from the movie. Three I reflected upon are:

WE ARE ALL ON THE PILGRIMAGE OF LIFE.

> Our pilgrimage is walking this road of life on earth until the Lord calls us home to heaven. We all have different starting points and times, as well as ending ones. Each of our pilgrimages takes different roads, consisting of twists, bumps, hills, and potholes along the way. Our ending destination is of paramount importance, not particularly the specific roads we travel.
>
> One thing that remains constant, though, is that God is leading each of our paths.
>
> > *"You make known to me the path of life; you*
> > *will fill me with joy in your presence,*
> > *with eternal pleasures at your right hand."*
> > ~ Psalm 16:11

Along the way, we meet many pilgrims.

During our pilgrimage, we meet many pilgrims who help shape and mold our lives. We have the honor of knowing some of them for a long time and some for a short season. One universal truth is that we all have our baggage, pain, and struggles. When we realize we are similar, we can extend Jesus' love, compassion, and mercy to our fellow pilgrims. A listening ear and an understanding heart can bring healing and grace. We can help others grow deeper in their relationship with Christ. We all need each other.

One thing that remains constant is that we were made for relationships. First, a relationship with Christ as the cornerstone, and then with others.

*"Jesus replied: 'Love the Lord your God with all
your heart and with all your soul
and with all your mind.' This is the first and greatest commandment.
And the second is like it: 'Love your neighbor as yourself.'"*
~ Matthew 22:37-39

We learn lessons daily on this pilgrimage.

Our goal on this pilgrimage is to journey closer to God and become the people He intends us to be. We should strive to become more like Him. Helping other pilgrims on their journey is the other goal. Through the different events in our lives, we can learn lessons that help us grow in faith and trust. We also learn from other pilgrims. They can encourage us, and we can do the same for them. Our hearts can soften, and we will be better reflections of Jesus when we take the time to see what God is teaching us. How is He revealing Himself through the events of our lives and as we take time to be still with Him?

One thing that remains constant is that we continue to grow in Christ.

"...We continually ask God to fill you with the knowledge of his will through all the wisdom and understanding that the Spirit gives, so that you may live a life worthy of the Lord and please him in every way: bearing fruit in every good work, growing in the knowledge of God."
~ Colossians 1:9-10

Take a few minutes to reflect on your pilgrimage.

> Are you following the path God intends for you?
> Are relationships above the things of this world?
> Is your relationship with God first in your life?
> Are you learning and growing closer to Christ?

Be encouraged to take a step toward growth in any area you feel God is calling you. Call to Him, and He will guide your path.

"Difficult roads often lead to beautiful destinations. The best is yet to come."
~ Zig Ziglar

"Those who walk with God, always reach their destination."
~ Henry Ford

"We're all just walking each other home."
~ Ram Dass

REFLECTION:

What pilgrim has had the most impact on your pilgrimage?
Is Christ first in your life?

"'Which of these three do you think proved to be a neighbor to the man who fell into the robbers' hands?' And he said, 'The one who showed compassion to him.' Then Jesus said to him, 'Go and do the same.'"
~ Luke 10:36-37 (NASB)

12

The Blessing of Ministry

One of the many blessings we, as Christians, have is the gift of ministry that Jesus so beautifully personified in His life.

Have you ever noticed how He was always reaching out to the lost, the lowly, and the sick? He had compassion for them and wanted to heal and help them. Shouldn't we follow His example?

Do you find joy or happiness when you are ministering to others? I am happiest when I can assist others. Our ministry can have a ripple effect, bless others, and inspire others to do more.

What are some different ministries?
- Working at a soup kitchen.
- Serving food at a bereavement ministry.
- Reading books to children at the library.
- Sending cards to the lonely or sick.
- Sponsoring a child in another country to help them get an education.
- Sincerely and faithfully praying for people who are sick or in need of special prayer.
- Bringing food to the shut-ins.
- Giving money to people in need.
- Paying for someone's coffee anonymously.
- Visiting a widow or widower.
- Helping little ones and their teacher at school.
- Making pies for your Bible study prayer partners.

There are so many different things that can be considered ministry. If you are doing it to give honor and glory to God and because of what He has done in your life, I think it qualifies as ministry.

When I was a teen, I enjoyed volunteering at the local hospital. It was then that I started to learn the joy of helping others. Meeting people who couldn't do things for themselves because of either physical disabilities or being sick enabled me to help others and opened a whole new world.

I remember helping my grandmother and great-aunt as a teen. My great aunt's eyes failed as she aged, so I became her eyes, taking care of her paperwork and finances. As a young adult, I helped with our church's youth group because some older friends encouraged me. I enjoyed helping in little ways at youth group retreats and different functions.

When my children ranged in age from 1½ to 9 years old, I felt a calling to do some type of family ministry. I contacted a church, and we were paired with a couple who graciously accepted our family as helpers at a soup kitchen. Often, my youngest child would be sleeping on my shoulder as we helped prepare and serve the food. I found myself praying for the people as we served them, asking God to meet their needs and provide for them.

I enjoyed volunteering at a school for a few hours a week, helping the teacher and the children. They were such a joy to watch, seeing their innocence and the love they shared. Some years, the children were so friendly, hugging me or taking my hand to walk somewhere with them. It was always a blessing to pray for them and to think about their future.

My favorite ministry through the years has been holding babies in the NICU. It is so special to try to comfort and love the little ones who need that extra tender loving care.

I encourage you to continually think of and seek ways to minister to others. Your life will be blessed in unexpected ways, as well as blessing other people.

REFLECTION:

What has been your favorite ministry?
What non-traditional ministry has brought you joy?

> *"Jesus saw the huge crowd as he stepped from the boat, and he had compassion on them and healed their sick."*
> ~ Matthew 14:14 (NLT)

13

Building Trust

"Anything that's human is mentionable, and anything that is mentionable can be more manageable. When we can talk about our feelings, they become less overwhelming, less upsetting, and less scary. The people we trust with that important talk can help us know that we are not alone."
~ Fred Rogers

The music director of a church congregation shared the above quote. He was having surgery for cancer the following day. What wisdom can we glean from the quote?

It reminded me of the importance of…

>creating a safe space for honest conversation.
>listening with our hearts.
>being trustworthy.
>being available to encourage.
>not letting people walk alone.

While reflecting on the quote, I couldn't help but think how God is the perfect model for us. When we turn to God in our brokenness as we go through trials or when life's problems seem to overwhelm us, He…

>welcomes us in the safety of His arms as we share our hearts with Him.

"His huge outstretched arms protect you— under them you're perfectly safe;
his arms fend off all harm."
~ Psalm 91:4 (MSG)

listens to us with His heart.

"Then you will call on me and come and pray to me,
and I will listen to you."
~ Jeremiah 29:12

lets us know we can trust Him.

"Trust in him at all times, you people;
pour out your hearts to him, for God is our refuge."
~ Psalm 62:8

sends us encouragement, be it a blessing in nature or a passage in the Word.

"For I am the Lord your God who takes hold of your right hand
and says to you, Do not fear; I will help you."
~ Isaiah 41:13

assures us He is with us.

"Have I not commanded you? Be strong and courageous.
Do not be frightened, and do not be dismayed, for the
Lord your God is with you wherever you go."
~ Joshua 1:9 (ESV)

What a treasure it is in our lives when, especially in our distress, we first turn to God to share with Him. Knowing that God is always there for us, listening, comforting, and encouraging us, gives us true peace. As we trust the Lord more and more, we realize we are never alone. God is with us in the most difficult of circumstances.

It is always an extra blessing to see the people God puts in our path who model those godly attributes in the human form. Sometimes we need that human connection to feel God's grace even more in our lives.

I will leave you with this quote from a sermon…

> "It is in the respect and honor
> that we hold others
> that we most praise God."

May you be encouraged to…

> reach out to God and share your heart when life is tough, and you need a reminder that you are not alone.
> look for faithful, trustworthy humans who will be there when you need them.
> seek ways you can improve yourself in building trust with others.
> praise God by the way you respect and honor those in your path by meeting their needs.

REFLECTION:

Who provides godly encouragement for you?
Who comes to you knowing you are there for them?

> *"The Lord is merciful and compassionate,*
> *slow to get angry and filled with unfailing love."*
> ~ Psalm 145:8 (NLT)

14

Unity In Prayer

God uses every detail in our lives to provide His perfect orchestration of our steps. One day, a sequence of events led me to arrive earlier than usual at church. I was in my pew praying and turned to get something out of my bag. I looked up and saw a woman I had never seen before. She asked, "Would you please pray for my heartbroken son? You seem like you must be a good pray-er to be at church so early." She then shared more details so I would know how to pray for her son and the situation. I felt inspired to give her a copy of my book, *God's Presence Illuminated*, hoping it might encourage her. She seemed delighted and said, "Well, it must have been the Holy Spirit that prompted me to share with you. Thank you so much." I asked if I could hug her and she said, "Sure."

Reflecting on this ordained God moment, I felt I could relate to what this woman was experiencing on a few levels.

Have you ever been so desperate in prayer, crying out to Jesus?
> Perhaps you needed to share a heavy burden with both a human and God.

> *"A woman in the crowd had suffered for twelve years with constant bleeding. She had suffered a great deal from many doctors, and over the years she had spent everything she had to pay them, but she had gotten no better. In fact, she had gotten worse. She had heard about Jesus, so she came up behind him through the crowd and touched his robe. For she thought to herself, 'If I can just touch his robe, I will be healed.'"*
> ~ Mark 5:25-28 (NLT)

Imagine the desperation the woman felt. She suffered greatly, being shunned by people and deemed ceremonially unclean for twelve years. The woman spent all her money seeking help but to no avail. She got worse. She was desperate and had faith in Jesus after hearing about Him. He could heal her. All she had to do was touch the hem of His robe.

When have you felt such desperation that you wanted to touch the hem of Jesus' robe?

Spending time in quiet prayer lends itself to touching the hem of Jesus' robe.

Have you been heartbroken?

Were there some friends to comfort you?

> *"When Jesus arrived at Bethany, he was told that Lazarus had already been in his grave for four days. Bethany was only a few miles down the road from Jerusalem, and many of the people had come to console Martha and Mary in their loss. When Martha got word that Jesus was coming, she went to meet him. But Mary stayed in the house. Martha said to Jesus, 'Lord, if only you had been here, my brother would not have died. But even now I know that God will give you whatever you ask.' Jesus told her, 'Your brother will rise again.'"*
> ~ John 11:17-23 (NLT)

> *"When Mary arrived and saw Jesus, she fell at his feet and said, 'Lord, if only you had been here, my brother would not have died.' When Jesus saw her weeping and saw the other people wailing with her, a deep anger welled up within him, and he was deeply troubled. 'Where have you put him?' he asked them. They told him, 'Lord, come and see.' Then Jesus wept."*
> ~ John 11:32-35 (NLT)

Martha and Mary were heartbroken at the death of their brother, Lazarus. They both had friends to console them. Martha and Mary, at separate times, expressed their disappointment and brokenheartedness to Jesus that, had He been present, Lazarus would not have died. Jesus wept too.

When have you been so heartbroken you wanted Jesus to be physically present to make everything better?

> Being honest with the Lord brings us into a closer presence with Him, especially when we are heartbroken.

Have you needed the faith of others to carry you when you felt helpless?

> *"And when he (Jesus) returned to Capernaum after some days, it was reported that he was at home. And many were gathered together, so that there was no more room, not even at the door. And he was preaching the word to them. And they came, bringing to him a paralytic carried by four men. And when they could not get near him because of the crowd, they removed the roof above him, and when they had made an opening, they let down the bed on which the paralytic lay. And when Jesus saw their faith, he said to the paralytic, 'Son, your sins are forgiven.'"*
> ~ Mark 2:1-5 (ESV)

> *"'I say to you, rise, pick up your bed, and go home.' And he rose and immediately picked up his bed and went out before them all, so that they were all amazed and glorified God, saying, 'We never saw anything like this!'"*
> ~ Mark 2:11-12 (ESV)

What perseverance this paralytic's friends had. They were determined to bring their friend to Jesus and came up with a clever way to get him to see Jesus despite the huge crowd. Notice that it was the faith of the paralytic's friends that Jesus saw, as it says, *"When Jesus saw **their** faith."* Because of his friends' faith, Jesus forgave the paralytic's sins and healed him.

When has your faith wavered and grown weak and you needed your friends' faith to bring you to Jesus for His healing touch?

> Sharing a prayer need with trusted friends yokes us together and strengthens our faith.

May you be reminded of the importance of…

> unity in prayer, the privilege we have.
> reaching out to the Body of Christ in your desperation.
> comforting the brokenhearted.
> knowing God is close to the brokenhearted.
> your friends and their faith.
> staying yoked with Jesus.

REFLECTION:

How did Jesus provide healing when you reached out to touch the hem of His garment?
When has the faith of your friends carried you to Jesus?

> *"Carry each other's burdens, and in this way*
> *you will fulfill the law of Christ."*
> ~ Galatians 6:2

15

Paid In Full

> *"She will give birth to a son, and you are to give him the name Jesus, because he will save his people from their sins."*
> ~ Matthew 1:21

Jesus is the greatest gift of all time. I am grateful for a different kind of Christmas gift I received one year. I stopped at a local hometown pharmacy that also sells Christian items to ask about selling copies of my books there. The owner said they like to support local people and do not charge a commission, as most places do. After looking at the book, he said they would be glad to take five of them to sell.

When I brought the books in, he immediately wrote me a check for the cost of the five books. He decided to gift me by paying upfront for the books, not even considering he might incur a loss if the books did not sell. That, to me, was a special Christmas gift.

He said even though the pharmacy is their business, their greatest pleasure is in seeing people's joy in sharing when they find the perfect item such as a Christian card, gift, or book. Sharing the gospel message is an important part of their business, and they like to support others who have that same mission.

As I watched him write the check and share those thoughts with me, I could not help but think about the significance and parallel of Jesus' birth over 2000 years ago.

On the first Christmas, Jesus, conceived by the Holy Spirit, was born of a woman. Jesus' birth began God's plan of salvation for all humanity. The most special Christmas gift that God provided for us is Jesus' life. Through Jesus' birth, life on earth, death on the cross, and resurrection, Jesus paid for our salvation upfront. Jesus paid it in full.

God took a chance on us, hoping that **we** would accept Jesus as our Lord and Savior and spend eternity in heaven. We have forgiveness for our sins and access to God's grace.

Consider these verses, which speak of how Jesus paid for our salvation. Take a few minutes to reflect on the significance of each one, thanking Jesus for the gift He paid for you and your salvation.

"For even the Son of Man came not to be served but to serve others and to give his life as a ransom for many."
~ Mark 10:45 (NLT)

"For the wages of sin is death, but the free gift of God is eternal life in Christ Jesus our Lord."
~ Romans 6:23 (ESV)

"Don't you realize that your body is the temple of the Holy Spirit, who lives in you and was given to you by God? You do not belong to yourself, for God bought you with a high price. So you must honor God with your body."
~ 1 Corinthians 6:19-20 (NLT)

"For there is one God, and there is one mediator between God and men, the man Christ Jesus, who gave himself as a ransom for all, which is the testimony given at the proper time."
~ 1 Timothy 2:5-6 (ESV)

REFLECTION:

Have you accepted the gift of Christ as your Lord and Savior?
Have you thanked Jesus for paying for your salvation?

> *"'Today in the town of David a Savior has been born to you; he is the Messiah, the Lord. This will be a sign to you: You will find a baby wrapped in cloths and lying in a manger.' Suddenly a great company of the heavenly host appeared with the angel, praising God and saying, 'Glory to God in the highest heaven, and on earth peace to those on whom his favor rests.'"*
> ~ Luke 2:11-14

16

Connections

A new friend was excited to share a powerful story of Mister Rogers' influence on his life through the years. He suggested we meet in person for the first time to talk. I was honored to listen, and I cried and smiled as I saw God at work in his life.

I could see the influence of Mister Rogers flowing out of him through the way he lives. This man, through the years, has learned the importance of caring about the people he meets, both professionally and personally.

He lives knowing the value of...

> making connections with people.
> caring about others, asking them, "Who are you?" and taking time to know the core of their being.
> getting people in touch with themselves and others.

In retrospect, I can't help but see how powerful and perfect a quote he shared in an email:

"If you could only sense how important you are to the lives of those you meet; how important you can be to the people you may never even dream of. There is something of yourself that you leave at every meeting with another person."
~ Fred Rogers

He also said, "And I guess our encounter with one another left a lasting impression on both of us." I saw God's ripple effect of goodness with this man sharing his story at church the first day, which inspired me to hand him a copy of my book, telling him I would be praying for him. It has led to an unexpected friendship that is blessing us both, and as he also said, "Unexpected friends are the best."

> *"When one of the Pharisees invited Jesus to have dinner with him, he went to the Pharisee's house and reclined at the table. A woman in that town who lived a sinful life learned that Jesus was eating at the Pharisee's house, so she came there with an alabaster jar of perfume. As she stood behind him at his feet weeping, she began to wet his feet with her tears. Then she wiped them with her hair, kissed them and poured perfume on them. When the Pharisee who had invited him saw this, he said to himself, 'If this man were a prophet, he would know who is touching him and what kind of woman she is— that she is a sinner.'"*
> ~ Luke 7:36-39

> *"Then he turned toward the woman and said to Simon, 'Do you see this woman? I came into your house. You did not give me any water for my feet, but she wet my feet with her tears and wiped them with her hair. You did not give me a kiss, but this woman, from the time I entered, has not stopped kissing my feet. You did not put oil on my head, but she has poured perfume on my feet. Therefore, I tell you, her many sins have been forgiven— as her great love has shown. But whoever has been forgiven little loves little.' Then Jesus said to her, 'Your sins are forgiven.'"*
> ~ Luke 7:44-48

I don't think the woman in this story ever dreamed she would meet Jesus face-to-face. I doubt she knew her encounter with Jesus would have the impact it did on both of their lives. Jesus did not shun this woman, a sinner, as the Pharisee called her. This woman even did what the "religious" host should have done but didn't. She anointed and cleaned the feet of Jesus, making Him feel honored and welcome. Her act of sharing love with Jesus led Him to give her the unexpected gift of forgiving her sins. Both the woman and Jesus had a lasting effect on each other's lives.

Would you live your life any differently if you took this quote to heart?

"If you could only sense how important you are to the lives of those you meet; how important you can be to the people you may never even dream of. There is something of yourself that you leave at every meeting with another person."
~ Fred Rogers

As you go about your day, whether…

> going to work,
> running errands,
> staying home with the family,
> or doing ministry…

Do you sense how important you are to the lives of those you meet?

At times, we get so busy doing things that we need a reminder that relationships are most important. Each interaction we have in our day is an opportunity to share God's love. We might think our interaction is so small and not important, but we never know how God will use it to impact another's life.

Maybe the stranger you smiled at in the store lives alone and has no one to visit them.
Maybe sending a text to a person telling them you were praying for them saved their life.
Maybe a new friendship speaking life into your spirit gave you the encouragement you needed to step out in faith.

How important you can be to the people you may never even dream of?

We never know the orchestrations God has planned for our lives. We might meet a person in a completely different social class who comes into our lives to help us understand others more. Blessings abound when we are open to unexpected friendships.

Have you ever prayed for God to bring a new relationship into your life?
Have you asked God for a Christian friend so you can talk about spiritual things?
Have you seen the blessings of unexpected friendships?

How there is something of yourself that you leave at every meeting with another person?

With every interaction with people, we leave a part of ourselves with them. Sometimes that part of us can be something good, and sometimes bad. We influence others all the time without even knowing it.

Are you striving to share God's love and goodness?
Do you share more encouragement than negativity?
Do others see your attentiveness in listening to them?

> *"There is something of yourself
> that you leave
> at every meeting
> with another person."*

I see God working in my life through my writing ministry as I meet new people through the sharing of my books. God is expanding my world, and the forming of more spiritual friendships is enriching my life. It is a privilege to learn people's stories and see the blessings God orchestrates. Strangers quickly become friends in the Lord.

May you be encouraged to…

> know your life is valuable to others.
> be open to people you never thought of friending before.

leave a bit of yourself, along with God's love and goodness, with everyone you meet.

make connections with people.

care about others and ask "Who are you?" as you take the time to know the core of their being.

get people in touch with themselves and others.

love others.

forgive more.

share God's grace.

REFLECTION:

Do you need to slow down a little and show more care and compassion to make others feel valued?
Who has enriched your life by taking the time to learn your story?

> *"Is there any encouragement from belonging to Christ? Any comfort from his love? Any fellowship together in the Spirit? Are your hearts tender and compassionate? Then make me truly happy by agreeing wholeheartedly with each other, loving one another, and working together with one mind and purpose."*
> ~ Philippians 2:1-2 (NLT)

17

Appreciation

"I appreciate you."

Three simple words, yet so powerful! They were the parting words from the cashier, as I finished paying for my purchase at a local Dollar General store. Frankly, it surprised me. I don't think a cashier has ever said that to me before. As I walked to my car and got inside, ready to start the engine, those three words echoed in my mind. They prompted me to go back into the store with one of my books in tow.

I said, "This is a little strange, but I was wondering if you would like this book," showing it to her. Her face lit up when she saw it and a huge smile came over her countenance. I said, "You can use it as a 90-day devotional." She said, "That is just perfect. I like devotionals. We are new to the area and are adjusting to life here." As I walked away, the cashier again said, "I appreciate you."

I smiled and left the store with joy in my heart, in awe of God's perfect orchestration. You see, it started with the simple act of wanting to send a sympathy card to a man I met a few times who lives an hour and a half away from me. I did not realize his wife, with whom a mutual friend shared my first book, had died a few weeks earlier. Later, I met her and gave her my second book. I was surprised when, one day, she got my cell phone number from our mutual friend. We had a lovely conversation when she called to say how grateful she was for the books and encouraged me to keep writing.

On this particular day, I was running a few errands before I met a friend for coffee. I planned to go to a different Dollar General later in the day. Since I was a few minutes early, I put Dollar General in my GPS to see which one was closest. Much to my surprise, I had forgotten about the one closest to where I was. Only God, in His perfect orchestrations, could work all of those little details out for His glory.

While reflecting on this encounter, three main thoughts came to mind.

TO ALWAYS BE IN AWE OF GOD.

> *"I have heard all about you, Lord. I am filled with awe by your amazing works. In this time of our deep need, help us again as you did in years gone by. And in your anger, remember your mercy."*
> ~ Habakkuk 3:2 (NLT)

Once again, I was in awe of God, thinking about how He worked so many little details to orchestrate that divine moment. He is truly amazing in how He does it.

How many times does God…

> orchestrate the perfect events in our lives?
> save us from danger?
> work things out for our good?
> use us to minister in the life of someone else?
> brighten our days through a simple act of kindness we do for someone?
> use us to spread kindness to a stranger, perhaps without even realizing it?

Do you take time to be in awe of God working in you and your life, and thank Him for His goodness?

To tell people, with sincerity, "I appreciate you."

> *"I thank my God every time I remember you."*
> ~ Philippians 1:3

Think about the people you encounter in a day…

> family and friends.
> people in your church community.
> postal workers.
> servers at restaurants.
> pastors.
> prayer warriors.
> teachers.
> coworkers.

Do you…

> take time to think about the gifts they share?
> thank them for the encouragement they provide?
> appreciate the uniqueness that God created in everyone?

Do you tell the people in your life that you appreciate and value the gift they are to you?

To tell God, our Abba, with sincerity, "I appreciate you!"

> *"Praise the Lord! Give thanks to the Lord, for he is good! His faithful love endures forever."*
> ~ Psalm 106:1 (NLT)

Think about what life would be like without God.

If God were not real…

> our lives would have no purpose.
> we would not experience love.
> miracles would not happen.

Everything we have in this life and for eternity is because of God!

God has provided us with…

> the air we breathe.
> the food we eat.
> the people who are community to us.
> all of nature to enjoy.
> the ability to think.
> the ways we experience love and joy.

Is your life a reflection of your gratitude to God for all He has given you and all that you are? His Spirit and breath of life is in you.

Be encouraged to…

> be in awe and thankfulness for God's orchestrations in your life.
> use the phrase "I appreciate you!" to show your sincere, heartfelt gratitude to people.
> tell God how much you appreciate everything He has given to you.
> tell God how much you appreciate Him living in you.

> *"Being told you're appreciated*
> *is one of the simplest*
> *and most uplifting things*
> *you can hear."*
> ~ Sue Fitzmaurice

I hope you hear the sincerity in my voice when I say to you, my dear reader, *"I appreciate you!"*

I am grateful to be on this journey of life with you.

REFLECTION:

Which of the three thoughts above do you need to work on? Who can you sincerely tell, "I appreciate you"?

> *"I will praise you, Lord, with all my heart;*
> *I will tell of all the marvelous things you have done."*
> ~ Psalm 9:1 (NLT)

18

Holy Encounters

My spirit is renewed through experiencing holy encounters. These happened while I was attending a day retreat at one of my holy places on Canandaigua Lake. This place is like home to me. As soon as I walk in, I am greeted with friendly hellos from all the staff.

Out of the fifty people present, I noticed how God had my path cross a few times with a college-aged man. I first saw him after walking in and again before the retreat started as he walked past me.

At the first break, I felt inclined to share a copy of my book with the speaker, as much of what he shared seemed related. At the second break, I felt I should give a copy to this college-aged man, as it was refreshing to see a young person interested in growing in his faith. He commented that he was interested in checking out my book after the speaker had graciously shared about it. After giving the young man the book, he said he would be praying for me. It touched me when he said that. Here we were, two strangers, and he was going to be praying for me.

I took my time arriving for lunch and saw what seats were left as I did not know anyone on the retreat. It happened that there was a spot available at the young man's table. I thought it would be nice to talk with him and learn his story. The two other men at the table made me feel welcome also.

What a blessing to have four people come together as strangers, yet bonded in faith as children of God. The other two men wanted to learn more about me when they realized I was the author of the book. I was able to share some of my heart and faith journey with them. They both wanted a copy of the book, which I was able to give them. One is hoping to be able to use some thoughts to help him as he preaches the Word.

Since I was sitting next to the young man, it was easiest to converse with him. I was in awe of the wisdom and insights he shared and the encouragement a total stranger could breathe into my life. I feel he is wise beyond his years, and I am sure the Lord has great plans for him.

One man from my lunch table saw me on the way out, shook my hand, and said, "Safe travels. It was a pleasure meeting you. You are someone very special."

The final holy encounter was God sending me a heart stone while walking outside, reminding me of His great love for me.

As I took time to reflect on the day and the holy encounters, I was reminded of the truth of this verse:

> *"Keep on loving each other as brothers and sisters. Don't forget to show hospitality to strangers, for some who have done this have entertained angels without realizing it!"*
> ~ Hebrews 13:1-2 (NLT)

This passage reminds me of the importance of loving everyone because of God's love for us. We need to show love and welcome even the strangers we encounter each day. We never know how God will use a simple interaction to further His kingdom. Sincerely caring for those in our path can have an eternal impact. We are the Body of Christ, which God uses to share and encourage others. You may be the "angel" God uses to speak life to others.

Experiencing the holy encounters reminded me of the importance of...

>coming together with the Body of Christ.
>living together as brothers and sisters united in Christ.

being welcoming and caring.
listening to others with our ears and hearts.
being open to speaking words of life into the lives of others.
sharing God working in our lives with others.

REFLECTION:

How have you experienced the hospitality of a stranger?
How have you entertained an angel?

> *"... My heart is torn within me, and my compassion overflows."*
> ~ Hosea 11:8 (NLT)

19

The Blessed Caregivers

Caregivers deserve a special shout-out, and they need to know what a blessing they are. Through Bible study, I learned of a gentleman who had been battling cancer for four years. I felt compelled to visit him and his wife, though it was outside my comfort zone.

Doing something outside of ourselves and our comfort zone can be scary, but I am finding that I need to follow that little prompting and step out in faith. I kept debating if I could be brave enough to call them to see if they were open to a visit. I wondered what we would talk about if I visited. Thankfully, I mustered the courage to call, not just once, but twice, as nobody answered the first time. The wife was more than happy to accept an invitation for a visit, and so I was off to their house the next morning. She used to babysit my eldest child about 18 years earlier. I had not seen them in many years.

I brought some cookies for them, which they greatly appreciated. She made coffee, and even though at times I felt like maybe my words didn't come out right, I know the visit meant a lot to them. We had a wonderful time catching up on our lives, reminiscing about the old days, and being together. More than three hours flew by before I left.

During my visit, I was blessed to see the two of them interact, as well as with one of their daughters who was home helping them. It made me realize once again how special the role of a caregiver is and the extreme sacrifices they make. The caregivers I know personally care for their loved ones with such love and devotion.

I've witnessed caregivers serving their loved ones with…

> respect.
> dignity.
> love.
> patience.
> gentleness.
> kindness.
> faithfulness.
> words of endearment.

I know caregivers often sacrifice their wants and desires to be there for their loved ones. Many times, the caregiver cannot just go somewhere when they want because they cannot leave their loved one alone. This can be draining on the caregiver, but they continue to give us a great example. It truly is a special person who cares for another with such a humble and loving spirit. What a true example of being Christ to their loved one.

So, I would like to thank the blessed caregivers who give so much of themselves for their loved ones. They have touched my heart, and I know they are following Jesus' humble example of serving others.

REFLECTION:

Do you know of a caregiver who could use your encouragement to let them know you see their love and sacrifice?
Could you offer an hour or two of your time to give a caregiver a break?

> *"Light shines in the darkness for the godly.*
> *They are generous, compassionate, and righteous."*
> ~ Psalm 112:4 (NLT)

20

Rock Bottom

A huge smile came over my face when I saw an email with the subject line of "Immediately thought of you and smiled!" Needless to say, I was excited to read it, which I did right away. It was from a woman in Tennessee whom I have never met in person. We connected through social media.

Her email shared the following:

> She was moving some big stones to her flower bed.
> There were a total of eight stones, which were stacked four high by two across.
> The original stone pile was a perch for the watering cans she was using to draw rainwater, which she hadn't used in days.
> When she moved the seventh stone, this was what she saw on the lone, remaining stone.

> This stone had the only wet spot of any of the stones
> > on the very bottom of the piles
> > > under all the weight of the other stones
> > > > hidden from view
> > > > > there was a beautiful heart on the stone.

> Had she waited a little longer to move the stones,
> > most likely the wet spot would have evaporated.

I found her thoughts about our relationship with God and finding this heart insightful. She said,

> "Kind of reminds me of where we as mankind usually end up finding God…
> after we've exhausted ourselves from moving our "stones" around… and reach rock bottom…
> underneath all our struggles and faults and failures and attempts to do it alone…
> and all other manners of works of the flesh…
> that we find Jesus…
> just waiting for us to finally see His LOVE for us before it's too late!"

When we think about hitting rock bottom, it can happen before we come to know Christ in a personal way, or it can happen at any time in our relationship with Jesus. My thoughts turned to Peter, also called Simon, one of Jesus' original disciples.

> *"'Simon, Simon, Satan has asked to sift all of you as wheat. But I have prayed for you, Simon, that your faith may not fail. And when you have turned back, strengthen your brothers.' But he replied, 'Lord, I am ready to*

go with you to prison and to death.' Jesus answered, 'I tell you, Peter, before the rooster crows today, you will deny three times that you know me.'"
~ Luke 22:31-34

Isn't it comforting to know that Jesus knew Satan would try to get Peter to come to a place of spiritual ruin and, because of this, Jesus prayed for him? Jesus knew that Peter would return to the Lord and be called to strengthen the other disciples too. Peter was sure he would never stray from Jesus and was willing to face death for His sake.

"Then seizing him (Jesus), they led him away and took him into the house of the high priest. Peter followed at a distance. And when some there had kindled a fire in the middle of the courtyard and had sat down together, Peter sat down with them. A servant girl saw him seated there in the firelight. She looked closely at him and said, 'This man was with him.' But he denied it. 'Woman, I don't know him,' he said. A little later someone else saw him and said, 'You also are one of them.' 'Man, I am not!' Peter replied. About an hour later another asserted, 'Certainly this fellow was with him, for he is a Galilean.' Peter replied, 'Man, I don't know what you're talking about!' Just as he was speaking, the rooster crowed. The Lord turned and looked straight at Peter. Then Peter remembered the word the Lord had spoken to him: 'Before the rooster crows today, you will disown me three times.' And he went outside and wept bitterly."
~ Luke 22:54-62

We see how short-lived Peter's good intentions of even facing death for Jesus were. Just as Jesus had said, Peter denied knowing Him three times that night. As Peter was denying Jesus for the third time, Jesus' look pierced Peter's heart and soul. Peter was truly remorseful and repented immediately as he wept bitterly.

"When Jesus came to the region of Caesarea Philippi, he asked his disciples, 'Who do people say the Son of Man is?' They replied, 'Some

say John the Baptist; others say Elijah; and still others, Jeremiah or one of the prophets.' 'But what about you?' he asked. 'Who do you say I am?' Simon Peter answered, 'You are the Messiah, the Son of the living God.' Jesus replied, 'Blessed are you, Simon son of Jonah, for this was not revealed to you by flesh and blood, but by my Father in heaven. And I tell you that you are Peter, and on this rock I will build my church, and the gates of Hades will not overcome it. I will give you the keys of the kingdom of heaven; whatever you bind on earth will be bound in heaven, and whatever you loose on earth will be loosed in heaven.' Then he ordered his disciples not to tell anyone that he was the Messiah."
~ Matthew 16:13-20

Simon Peter is the one who speaks up, knowing in his heart that Jesus is the Messiah, the one they have been waiting for. Jesus assures him that he is correct and that God has revealed the truth to him. Because of Simon's profession of Jesus' Lordship, Jesus changes Simon's name to Peter and says it is the rock upon which the church was built. The church has the keys of the kingdom of heaven and knows how to live, proclaiming Jesus and the forgiveness of sins.

Peter's profession of Jesus as the Messiah and Jesus' calling Peter the Rock both happen before Peter's denial and return to Jesus! What encouragement for us to know that Jesus, even when we mess things up big time, always offers forgiveness and love if we return to Him.

How often are we like Peter?

> We have the best intentions of going the distance with God, but get sidetracked?
> Under peer pressure, deny knowing the Lord?
> Truly repent of our wrongdoing?
> Know in our hearts that Jesus is the Lord of all?

Our actions result in a huge mistake, hurting ourselves or others?
Standing on the truth of Jesus as the one and true Messiah?

When we hit rock bottom, do we need encouragement to…

keep in mind that Jesus is praying for our faith not to fail?
see Jesus looking into our hearts and soul with eyes of love, causing us to repent?
remain steadfast in our faith, even though we fail in our humanity?

Be encouraged to…

follow Peter's example of the profession of Jesus' Lordship in your life.
hold firmly to Jesus when you are at rock bottom.
repent and return to Jesus when you have made a major mistake.
experience the many ways Jesus showers you with His love.

REFLECTION:

When have you hit rock bottom and encountered Jesus' love?
When have you experienced Jesus' eyes looking into the depths of your heart and soul?

> *"Yet this I call to mind and therefore I have hope:*
> *Because of the Lord's great love we are not*
> *consumed, for his compassions never fail.*
> *They are new every morning; great is your faithfulness."*
> ~ Lamentations 3:21-23

21

Daily Connection

Do you find that life seems so busy? It seems like the pace of life has picked up these days. Life changes so quickly and sometimes we need a reminder to make the most of every moment. God is present and working even in the simplest of interactions.

Do you find alone time to be with the Lord?

> How many times do you walk by your neighbor without taking time to interact?
> How many times do you walk by a stranger without a simple smile or hello?
> How many times do you reach out to others when you need encouragement?

I challenge you through
> the busyness of life
>> to remember that
>>> your relationship with
>>>> God and others
>>>>> should remain your
>>>>>> highest priority.

THE IMPORTANCE OF BEING CONNECTED TO GOD DAILY.

I see how my life has been abundantly enriched by spending time daily walking and praying with the Lord. It has brought me into a closer union with God. I began to experience His presence and love on a deeper level.

Jesus consistently took time daily to commune with God, His Father, too. We should follow His example.

> *"Come close to God, and God will come close to you.*
> *Wash your hands, you sinners; purify your hearts, for your*
> *loyalty is divided between God and the world."*
> ~ James 4:8 (NLT)

THE IMPORTANCE OF BEING CONNECTED TO OTHERS, THE BODY OF CHRIST, DAILY.

Upon arriving home, I saw one of my widow neighbors out with her cat. I wanted to get to my "to-do" list for the day, but the thought of talking with her crossed my mind. I shut the garage door and went into the house, but then decided it was more important to go and talk to her. As soon as she saw me, she reached out to hug me, and we held the embrace for a few moments, sharing God's love. It was the first time we did that. It was a blessed time as she shared some heartache and sadness she was experiencing. Often, when I talk to her, I can't help but smile as I take time to put another before myself.

Do you take the time to reach out to someone when you need some encouragement? Recently, I was processing some changes in my life in two different situations. I saw how God used three people to be instrumental in helping me deal with these changes.

> One was available to let me share, listening with both their ears and heart, offering encouragement and thoughts on the situation. Afterward, I felt at peace.

> One was ready to pray for me through the situation, offering inspiration in word, thought, and prayer.

The other recognized a change would be difficult and was available to make the transition easier by walking alongside me.

> *"Two people are better off than one, for they can help each other succeed. If one person falls, the other can reach out and help. But someone who falls alone is in real trouble."*
> ~ Ecclesiastes 4:9-10 (NLT)

May you be encouraged to take time daily…

> to commune with God.
> to commune with your neighbor or stranger.
> to let others commune with you.

We are all on this journey of life together. We are companions on this journey of life ~ reach out and make a difference in someone's life today.

REFLECTION:

Who can you take a few minutes to connect with?
Do you need to ask someone to help support you as you go through a difficult time?

> *"Let us think of ways to motivate one another to acts of love and good works. And let us not neglect our meeting together, as some people do, but encourage one another, especially now that the day of his return is drawing near."*
> ~ Hebrews 10:24-25 (NLT)

22

The Power Source

Our area has experienced sudden thunderstorms. The latest was a severe thunderstorm with 75+ mph winds at 9:45 p.m., which downed trees in the area and left us without power for almost a full day. Some people were without power for three days.

The grace of God kept me and my husband safe as we were traveling home from visiting friends when the storm came rushing in. A few minutes into the short drive, the lightning lit up the sky. As we turned onto one road, the sky opened with a torrential downpour and massive wind. The scariest part was not being able to see the road but seeing green tree debris in our path. I held my breath, hoping a tree did not come crashing down on us or the roadway. When we turned onto our road, the power immediately flashed off. It was a relief to have arrived home safely despite not having any power.

Have you experienced losing power for a day or longer? The worst I experienced was in the flood of 2011, being without power for almost five days.

Isn't it kind of eerie when it is night, and you don't have power? How many times do you walk into a room and flip the light switch out of habit?

When we are without power, life seems to be on hold. Most likely, the plans you had for the day will change suddenly.

You can't go about doing the things you usually do…

> no cooking food.
> no grabbing a cold drink from the fridge.
> no using a computer.
> no heat in the winter.
> no hot water for a shower.
> no ability to charge your cell phone.
> limited ability to flush toilets for those with wells.

Sometimes God has a sense of humor, doesn't He? I had just published my weekly reflection, "Dancing in the Rain." I got to practice dancing in the rain. I read a book with a flashlight. It was something I could do without power.

The following morning, I decided to go out, get something to eat, and take a walk while dwelling in God's presence near some water. It was then I thought about the only true power source in our lives that never goes out.

Our true power source is the
> Holy Spirit,
>> the third person of the Trinity,
>>> whom Jesus promised to send once He ascended.

> *"And now I will send the Holy Spirit, just as my Father promised. But stay here in the city until the Holy Spirit comes and fills you with power from heaven."*
> ~ Luke 24:49 (NLT)

This Scripture passage was after Jesus' resurrection when He appeared to the disciples who were behind locked doors. Jesus showed them His hands and feet to prove who He was. Jesus ate broiled fish in their presence. He opened the disciples' minds so they could understand the Scriptures. They were witnesses of all Jesus had endured and were being sent to continue proclaiming the good news. The Holy Spirit is the true power that comes from heaven.

> *"The Spirit of God, who raised Jesus from the dead, lives in you. And just as God raised Christ Jesus from the dead, he will give life to your mortal bodies by this same Spirit living within you."*
> ~ Romans 8:11 (NLT)

We can only be connected to the Holy Spirit through Jesus. He gives us the same power that raised Jesus from the dead. The Holy Spirit lives in us.

What are we able to do with the power source leading us?

TO BE WITNESSES SHARING JESUS.

> *"But you will receive power when the Holy Spirit comes upon you. And you will be my witnesses, telling people about me everywhere— in Jerusalem, throughout Judea, in Samaria, and to the ends of the earth."*
> ~ Acts 1:8 (NLT)

TO BE GUIDED TO WALK IN TRUTH.

> *"But when he, the Spirit of truth, comes, he will guide you into all the truth. He will not speak on his own; he will speak only what he hears, and he will tell you what is yet to come."*
> ~ John 16:13

TO BEAR FRUIT IN OUR LIVES.

> *"But the Holy Spirit produces this kind of fruit in our lives: love, joy, peace, patience, kindness, goodness, faithfulness, gentleness, and self-control. There is no law against these things!"*
> ~ Galatians 5:22-23 (NLT)

May you be encouraged to reflect on the true power source in your life. Stay plugged into the power supply. The Spirit is in you thanks to Jesus' resurrection.

May the Holy Spirit guide you to…

>be a witness sharing Jesus.
>walk in truth.
>bear fruit in your life.

REFLECTION:

Was there a time when the power source of the Holy Spirit gave you the ability to witness?
What fruits is the Spirit producing in your life?

> *"'And they will be mine,' says the Lord of armies,*
> *'on the day that I prepare my own possession,*
> *and I will have compassion for them just as a man has compassion*
> *for his own son who serves him.'"*
> ~ Malachi 3:17 (NASB)

Section 2

GOD'S COMPASSION ILLUMINATED IN SCRIPTURE

"I will recount the steadfast love of the Lord, the praises of the Lord, according to all that the Lord has granted us, and the great goodness to the house of Israel that he has granted them according to his compassion, according to the abundance of his steadfast love."
~ Isaiah 63:7 (ESV)

Scripture is full of examples of God's love and compassion for all of humanity. What an honor it is for us to have the Scriptures where we can read the many stories to help us understand God even better.

We, because of Scripture, can share the stories that bring glory and honor to the Lord as we praise Him. We see the fruit of Scripture that also applies to our daily lives.

God's compassion illuminated in Scripture.

"Love and compassion are necessities, not luxuries. Without them, humanity cannot survive."
~ Dalai Lama

23

Rainbows

As I started driving to my daily walking spot, it began to downpour. I kept going as it looked brighter in that direction. When I got out of my car, it was just sprinkling a little. I grabbed my big golf umbrella and started walking. After a few minutes, I put my umbrella up as the rain picked up. Without warning, I found myself walking with no umbrella for shelter as the wind blew it inside out.

I put on a sweatshirt to help keep me dry and waited a few minutes for the rain to slow down. I then started walking my usual route and noticed the sun coming out just as quickly as the rain had come. When I turned around, much to my surprise, there was a beautiful, thick, vibrantly colored rainbow. I was in awe of the beauty. This rainbow encounter lasted a good fifteen minutes.

The rest of my walk was filled with God continually showing me His love through His beautiful reminders. They came in the form of heart-shaped stones and heart pedals the storm forced off a tree. I was in awe of their beauty as well. The reminders made me smile at God and thank Him for His goodness, which is all around us.

Whenever I see a rainbow, I am always reminded of this passage,

> "I have placed my rainbow in the clouds. It is the sign of my covenant with you and with all the earth. When I send clouds over the earth, the rainbow will appear in the clouds, and I will remember my covenant with you and with all living creatures. Never again will the floodwaters destroy all life."
> ~ Genesis 9:13-15 (NLT)

God made this rainbow covenant with all the earth and us. He will never again destroy all life through flooding. What an amazing love God has for us. Seeing the rainbow reminded me of the storms and rainbows in our faith journey. How important it is to look for the rainbows in our storms. They might not necessarily be the way we expect them to be.

Storm:
> *Cancer or Chronic Disease*
> Rainbow:
> > *A miracle of healing or the support of friends.*

Storm:
> *An offense that lands you in jail.*
> Rainbow:
> > *Time alone where you find the Lord or a ministry to let you know that others care.*

Storm:
> *A child straying from the faith.*
> Rainbow:
> > *They return to the Lord or comfort, knowing God is in control and loves them even more than you do.*

Rainbows also represent God's glory and greatness.

> *"I saw that from what appeared to be his waist up he looked like glowing metal, as if full of fire, and that from there down he looked like fire; and brilliant light surrounded him. Like the appearance of a rainbow in the clouds on a rainy day, so was the radiance around him. This was the appearance of the likeness of the glory of the Lord. When I saw it, I fell facedown, and I heard the voice of one speaking."*
> ~ Ezekiel 1:27-28

The prophet Ezekiel had a vision of God calling him into service. He was overwhelmed with the vision and the presence of the Lord. Ezekiel saw a brilliant, radiant light around this person. It was equal to the beauty of a rainbow in the sky. Before Ezekiel's vision, God's glory was associated only with the Temple of Jerusalem. The Lord was now appearing to His exiled people in Babylon. Ezekiel saw the glory of the Lord returning.

> *"The one sitting on the throne was as brilliant as gemstones— like jasper and carnelian. And the glow of an emerald circled his throne like a rainbow."*
> ~ Revelation 4:3 (NLT)

John had a vision of heaven. He describes the one sitting on the throne as the reflected brilliance of precious stones, with an emerald rainbow around the throne. What splendor and beauty radiates from the one on the throne.

> *"Then I saw another mighty angel coming down from heaven. He was robed in a cloud, with a rainbow above his head; his face was like the sun, and his legs were like fiery pillars."*
> ~ Revelation 10:1

In this vision, the angel had a face illuminated like the sun. The angel was robed in a cloud with a rainbow above his head, showing the great covenant of the rainbow. God's glory prevails.

I encourage you to take time to reflect on the significance of the rainbow God has graced us with...

as a constant reminder of our Father's commitment and an unfailing promise of His unwavering relationship of love.

to remember in the storms of life, look for the rainbows that come in different forms.

to see and experience God's glory and goodness that surrounds us.

REFLECTION:

What significance does the rainbow have for you?
How does God reveal His love for you?

> *"'For a brief moment I abandoned you, but with deep compassion I will bring you back. In a surge of anger I hid my face from you for a moment, but with everlasting kindness I will have compassion on you,' says the Lord your Redeemer."*
> ~ Isaiah 54:7-8

24

The Storms

Let's look at a familiar Bible story about Jesus and His disciples. What can we learn and apply to our lives?

> *"One day Jesus said to his disciples, 'Let us go over to the other side of the lake.' So they got into a boat and set out. As they sailed, he fell asleep. A squall came down on the lake, so that the boat was being swamped, and they were in great danger. The disciples went and woke him, saying, 'Master, Master, we're going to drown!' He got up and rebuked the wind and the raging waters; the storm subsided, and all was calm. 'Where is your faith?' he asked his disciples."*
> ~ Luke 8:22-25

Does this story draw parallels to our lives?

I like Jesus' first statement, *"Let us go over to the other side of the lake."*

>Couldn't that represent Jesus taking us in a new direction with something in our life? Maybe a new path we've never been down?

It is interesting to note that *"they got into the boat."*

>The word "they" refers to Jesus and His disciples. What a great reminder for us to remember that Jesus is always with us in the boat. He is always with us on our journey through life.

What did Jesus do soon after their boat trip started?
> He fell asleep! Jesus fell asleep easily, trusting and knowing that no matter what happened, everything would be fine. What a good lesson we can all learn from.

What happened just when all seemed to be smooth sailing?
> A squall, a sudden violent gust of wind or localized storm usually bringing rain, came along.

Does that ring true in your life?
> All is well until a major crisis hits, maybe even more than one at a time, to try to get us stuck down.

How did the disciples react when they felt danger quickly overtaking them?
> They panicked!
> Do you, like the disciples, panic when the storms come?
> Do the waves come crashing over the boat in your life, making you think you, too, are in danger?

In their panic, what did the disciples do?
> They rushed to Jesus, waking Him to tell Him they were about to drown.
> Can you hear the fear in their voices?
> Do you run to Jesus when the storms of life are overtaking you?
> Do you tell Him how you feel and that you need His help? Can you relate?
> I love how Jesus did not panic. In contrast, He appeared to be calm throughout the storm. He slept through most of it. The storm didn't faze Him at all.

To calm the disciples, though, what did Jesus do?
> He got up and rebuked the wind and the raging waters.
> Jesus remained in control the whole time. Isn't it powerful that Jesus asked the disciples where their faith was?
> Do we let Jesus take care of the storms in our lives? Do we panic or fear, or do we have faith?

What can we personally take away from this scene?

> Jesus is with us in the middle of the storm.
> We need to not panic and trust Him.
> Our faith needs to be bigger than our fear.

REFLECTION:

Does a storm of yours come to mind where you knew Jesus was with you? When has your faith been bigger than your fear?

> *"Then they cried out to the Lord in their trouble, and he brought them out of their distress. He stilled the storm to a whisper; the waves of the sea were hushed. They were glad when it grew calm, and He guided them to their desired haven."*
> ~ Psalm 107:28-30

25

God – Our Provider

I love the God moments that He orchestrates in the simple circumstances of our days. He always provides for us. I am in awe of His goodness.

My day started with attending a funeral and then making a visit to the doctor. There were several different routes I could have taken home, but I felt I should go on the highway. I believe it was part of His divine plan. At the last minute, I decided to stop and get gas.

I looked up toward the convenience store to see a man, Ken, whom I've known for over 35 years but don't see often. I told him I was sorry for not following through on a promise I made to his daughter months earlier; a promise he was unaware of. The promise was, if Ken survived his latest ordeal, I would share the good news that God is still in the miracle business. Doctors did not think Ken was going to make it due to the complicated heart issues he was experiencing.

In 2019, Ken had two heart attacks, eight heart catheterizations, and three prostate surgeries. One heart attack happened when he was in the ICU, and they quickly wheeled him away to perform another heart catheterization. With the issues of his heart, we were all pleasantly surprised to see how God answered prayers. Ken pulled through despite the unfavorable odds. Many people were praying for him.

Ken continues to push through, a little slower than before, with some limitations, but he continues to play pickleball three times a week, walks anywhere from 16,000 - 20,000 steps a day, and works part-time despite being in his 70s. Getting short of breath more easily is one of the limitations where he has had to listen to his body.

God has continued to work miracles in Ken's life this past year, and I am so thankful we got to connect at the gas station. He has always been a huge inspiration in my faith journey, and it has been a blessing to know him and his wife all these years.

They are generous people, always willing to have a houseful of people over for Sunday dinners for fellowship. They continue to do ministry work, especially promoting a wonderful program called Young Life. My youngest son's life was hugely impacted by this program.

Yes, the path on the drive home was God's perfect timing to run into him at just the perfect moment; any other path home would not have yielded that opportunity.

May these thoughts remind you that God is still in the miracle business.

>   Rejoice in every moment.
>   Be grateful for every interaction with one another.
>   Share God's goodness with all you meet.

REFLECTION:

What miracle have you witnessed in your or someone else's life?
Do you continue to share the good news with others?

>   *"Publish his glorious deeds among the nations.*
>   *Tell everyone about the amazing things he does."*
>   ~ Psalm 96:3 (NLT)

26

Jesus' Baptism

> "John appeared, baptizing in the wilderness and proclaiming a baptism of repentance for the forgiveness of sins. And all the country of Judea and all Jerusalem were going out to him and were being baptized by him in the river Jordan, confessing their sins."
> ~ Mark 1:4-5 (ESV)

People were traveling more than 20 miles to be baptized in the Jordan River since that is its closest point to Jerusalem. John's message for people was to confess their sins, repent of their sins, and be baptized with water. They knew God would grant forgiveness if they turned from sin to righteousness.

> "Then Jesus came from Galilee to the Jordan to John, to be baptized by him. John would have prevented him, saying, 'I need to be baptized by you, and do you come to me?' But Jesus answered him, 'Let it be so now, for thus it is fitting for us to fulfill all righteousness.' Then he consented. And when Jesus was baptized, immediately he went up from the water, and behold, the heavens were opened to him, and he saw the Spirit of God descending like a dove and coming to rest on him; and behold, a voice from heaven said, 'This is my beloved Son, with whom I am well pleased.'"
> ~ Matthew 3:13-17 (ESV)

Why was it so significant that Jesus was baptized by John?

Jesus, being divine, was without sin, so there was no need for confession or repentance.

> *"And you know that Jesus came to take away
> our sins, and there is no sin in him."*
> ~ 1 John 3:5 (NLT)

So why was Jesus baptized?

> In obedience to God, His Father.
>
> To commemorate the start of His public ministry.
>
> To show Jesus was consecrated (dedicated to God and sacred) to God.
>
> To show that Jesus identified with mankind and his sin, becoming our substitute.
>
> To show He was the fulfillment of righteousness (the quality or state of being morally correct and justifiable) for our sins.

Thoughts to ponder about Jesus' baptism…

> Even though Jesus was without sin, He waited in line with sinners to be baptized. From the beginning of His public ministry, Jesus always identified with sinners.
>
> How symbolic to learn that the Jordan River, specifically the Dead Sea, which is at one end of the Jordan River, is the lowest point on earth.
>
> Jesus entered into the depths of the lowest part of the earth. Imagine Jesus being baptized, going to the very bottom of the earth loaded down with the burdens of all mankind's guilt on His shoulders. He laid them down in the depths of the Jordan River so we could be free.
>
> Jesus' baptism is the bridge between Jesus' birth and His death on the cross.

Christmas– Jesus' birth joins humanity and divinity; the Word became Flesh.

Baptism– Jesus takes on the worst of humanity with all our sins and brokenness; Jesus becomes accessible to us.

Easter– Jesus' resurrection means salvation and eternal life for believers, being His finished work.

THE TRINITY WAS PRESENT AT JESUS' BAPTISM.

(GOD THE FATHER, JESUS THE SON, AND THE HOLY SPIRIT)

God the Father said,

> *"This is my beloved Son,*
> *with whom I am well pleased."*

Jesus' identity was fully revealed. God gave His verbal affirmation to Jesus. Note that Jesus did not do any miracles or any form of ministry to earn God's affirmation of His beloved Son.

Jesus the Son.

> *"When Jesus was baptized, he immediately rose from the water,*
> *and the heavens were opened to Him."*

At His baptism, the heavens opened, showing the way to God for those who follow Jesus.

The Holy Spirit is often depicted as a dove.

> *"And he saw the Spirit of God*
> *descending like a dove and coming to rest on Him."*

How does Jesus' baptism apply to our lives?

We, too, need to…

> confess our sins and repent.
> be baptized.
> hear God say to us personally, "You are my beloved son/daughter with whom I am well pleased."
> own our identity as a beloved son/daughter.
> hear God, the Father, give His verbal approval to us.
> remember our love for God and Jesus is most important before any ministry work.
> know the Trinity resides in our lives– God, Jesus, and the Holy Spirit.

REFLECTION:

Do you see how powerful it was that Jesus was willing to be baptized? How do you live out your baptismal call, knowing the Trinity resides in you?

> *"See what kind of love the Father has given to us, that we should be called children of God; and so we are. The reason why the world does not know us is that it did not know him. Beloved, we are God's children now, and what we will be has not yet appeared; but we know that when he appears we shall be like him, because we shall see him as he is."*
> ~ 1 John 3:1-2 (ESV)

27

The Power of Thoughts

"Don't let your hearts be troubled. Trust in God, and trust also in me."
~ John 14:1 (NLT)

Jesus said these words to His disciples after telling them He would only be with them for a short time. He knew the appointed time for Him to return to God was coming quickly. While they waited to be reunited with Him in heaven, Jesus did not want their hearts to be troubled. They needed to trust God in everything. Jesus knew the disciples would be sad and scared of being alone, so He stressed the importance of trusting in God. He wanted them to have a positive attitude, trust Him, and not dwell on the negative.

This same message applies to you and me. Jesus does not want our hearts to be troubled. He encourages us to trust in God.

> How many times do our thoughts go to the past and the mistakes we have made?
> How often are our thoughts stuck on the what-ifs and the negatives?
> How often do we forget God's immeasurable love for us?

Our thoughts influence the way we live and how we view life. Our thoughts are like an airport control tower for our bodies. That is good news because we can choose what controls our thoughts. There are all kinds of messages and thoughts that bombard us.

What should we strive to think about?

> *"Think about the things of heaven, not the things of earth."*
> ~ Colossians 3:2 (NLT)

When we keep in mind that heaven is our true home, and the things of this world are only temporary, we can keep our thoughts focused on the eternal.

> *"You will keep in perfect peace all who trust in you, all whose thoughts are fixed on you!"*
> ~ Isaiah 26:3 (NLT)

When we consciously try to think about God and the promises He gives us through His Word, we experience perfect peace, and we grow in trust. God wants only the best for His children.

> *"Therefore do not be anxious about tomorrow, for tomorrow will be anxious for itself. Sufficient for the day is its own trouble."*
> ~ Matthew 6:34 (ESV)

Jesus is reinforcing the importance of keeping our thoughts and focus on the present day and time. We should take one moment at a time, be truly present, and not be anxious about tomorrow.

> *"We destroy arguments and every lofty opinion raised against the knowledge of God and take every thought captive to obey Christ."*
> ~ 2 Corinthians 10:5 (ESV)

This passage encourages us to know that even our thoughts should obey and focus on Christ. We have the power to seize and take control of our thoughts as Christ reigns victoriously in us. When ungodly thoughts threaten to overtake us, we need to bring them to Christ. He can help us filter our thoughts with God's Word and power in our lives.

We have the power to change our thoughts if they are not what they should be.

As you go about your day, consciously consider your thoughts…

> being proactive with your thoughts.
> being reminded of God's promises.
> being positive and trusting God.
> being at peace knowing God is in control.
> taking captive your thoughts, focusing on Christ.

REFLECTION:

Is there a certain area you need to work on to keep your thoughts more positive?
Do you need a reminder to turn your anxious thoughts over to God?

> *"Now may the Lord of peace himself give you his*
> *peace at all times and in every way.*
> *The Lord be with all of you."*
> ~ 2 Thessalonians 3:16

28

Joy and Sorrow

A friend shared a *New York Times* newspaper article, "What Mary Can Teach Us About the Joy and Pain of Life." I found it thought-provoking, having a few messages relevant to our lives.

It made me reflect on how life consists of both joy and sorrow.

Have you considered how joy and sorrow can even be present in the same event?

In a short version of the angel's announcement to Mary, we read,

> *"Gabriel appeared to her and said, 'Greetings, favored woman! The Lord is with you!' Confused and disturbed, Mary tried to think what the angel could mean. 'Don't be afraid, Mary,' the angel told her, 'for you have found favor with God! You will conceive and give birth to a son, and you will name him Jesus.'"*
> ~ Luke 1:28-31 (NLT)

Consider what joy and pain Mary must have experienced with the angel's greeting.

The angel's greeting is one of joy, as Gabriel shares that Mary is favored.

At the same time, we learn Mary was confused and disturbed, wondering what her life was going to be like. She was already pledged to be married to Joseph and had not had relations with any man.

> How would people view her?
> Would they believe she was a virgin?
> What would Joseph think?
> Would Joseph divorce her?

When Jesus was eight days old, Luke 1:21-40 shares the story of Jesus being presented in the temple. We know Simeon and Anna were both in the temple waiting for the *"redemption of Jerusalem,"* which they knew was Jesus. Simeon shared this message with Mary,

> *"Then Simeon blessed them and said to Mary, his mother: 'This child is destined to cause the falling and rising of many in Israel, and to be a sign that will be spoken against, so that the thoughts of many hearts will be revealed. And a sword will pierce your own soul too.'"*
> ~ Luke 2:34-35

What joy Mary must have experienced in hearing Simeon and Anna confirm what the angel Gabriel had foretold. But what she must have thought of the words,

> *"And a sword will pierce your own soul too."*

What pain and sorrow would she endure? With the word *"too,"* we hear for the first time in Luke's Gospel that Jesus would endure joy and sorrow as well.

In Luke 2:41-52, we read about when Jesus was twelve years old and went with Mary and Joseph to Jerusalem for the Feast of the Passover,

> *"Thinking he was in their company, they traveled on for a day. Then they began looking for him among their relatives and friends. When they did not find him, they went back to Jerusalem to look for him.*

> *After three days they found him in the temple courts, sitting among the teachers, listening to them and asking them questions."*
> ~ Luke 2:44-46

What joy Mary and the family must have experienced while traveling together and at the Feast of the Passover. How quickly sorrow must have overtaken them once they realized Jesus was not with them as they were traveling home. The trip back to the temple must have seemed like forever.

I have to think Simeon's telling Mary,

> *"A sword will pierce your own soul too,"*

ultimately referred to this passage,

> *"Standing near the cross were Jesus' mother, and his mother's sister, Mary (the wife of Clopas), and Mary Magdalene. When Jesus saw his mother standing there beside the disciple he loved, he said to her, 'Dear woman, here is your son.' And he said to this disciple, 'Here is your mother.' And from then on this disciple took her into his home."*
> ~ John 19:25-27 (NLT)

Mary must have been thinking back to the moment the angel announced her virgin birth and all the moments in Jesus' life, which she treasured in her heart. Mary experienced continuous moments of joy and sorrow with Jesus, just as we do in our lives. At the cross, I believe she experienced the joy of knowing the Son she birthed was truly the Savior of the world, setting all humankind free from the bondage of their sin. At the same time, Mary experienced the pure agony of seeing her Son bruised, tortured, and hanging on the cross. What a helpless feeling not to be able to help Him.

Jesus also experienced both joy and sorrow as He was hanging on the cross.

> *"Fixing our eyes on Jesus, the pioneer and perfecter of faith. For the joy set before him he endured the cross, scorning its shame, and sat down at the right hand of the throne of God."*
> ~ Hebrews 12:2

What a powerful thought. While sacrificing His life on the cross, Jesus endured both joy and sorrow. What agony Jesus endured as a result of the beatings He received and as He hung on the cross, waiting for His last breath. His joy of obedience to God's will was much greater than the suffering He endured. I am sure Jesus was not feeling joyful hanging on the cross, but He knew it had to be done so we could all live for eternity with God.

Ultimately, biblical joy can be defined as joy that is dependent on who God is rather than our circumstances or who we are. Remembering that God is over all circumstances in our lives can produce joy even when we don't feel joyful.

May you be encouraged to remember that...

> God is always present in both our joy and sorrow.
> obedience to God's will produces more joy than sorrow.
> our joy is solely dependent on who God is.

May these verses about joy and sorrow provide encouragement.

> *"For his anger lasts only a moment, but his favor lasts a lifetime! Weeping may last through the night, but joy comes with the morning."*
> ~ Psalm 30:5 (NLT)

> *"Our hearts ache, but we always have joy. We are poor, but we give spiritual riches to others.*

We own nothing, and yet we have everything."
~ 2 Corinthians 6:10 (NLT)

"Those who sow in tears shall reap with shouts of joy!"
~ Psalm 126:5 (ESV)

JOY
    has victory over
        SORROW
            because of
                who GOD is!

REFLECTION:

What event in your life brought both joy and sorrow?
Is your joy in life solely dependent on who God is?

"I have heard all about you, Lord. I am filled with awe by your amazing works. In this time of our deep need, help us again as you did in years gone by. And in your anger, remember your mercy."
~ Habakkuk 3:2 (NLT)

29

The Vineyard

God gives us beautiful images of the vine and the branches in the 15th chapter of John's Gospel. Let's take a deeper look at some of those verses and see what we can learn from them.

> *"I am the true grapevine, and my Father is the gardener."*
> ~ John 15:1 (NLT)

We know that Jesus is the true grapevine, that God is the gardener, and that we have the honor of being grapevine branches. Consider your heart as being a branch, an extension from the vine of Jesus. You are responsible for planting a vineyard with your life while on this earth. When you get to heaven, the fruit of your labor will be fully rewarded.

What types of seeds do you sow and harvest in your vineyard?

Sow fewer seeds of…

> pride.
> conflict.
> unforgiveness.
> anger.
> bitterness.
> envy.
> hatred.
> discord.
> jealousy.

Sow more seeds of…

> gratitude.
> kindness.
> joy.
> peace.
> encouragement.
> faithfulness.
> prayer.
> understanding.
> love.
> generosity.

Who makes the seeds in your vineyard produce good fruit?

God, our Father, is the gardener of our vineyard. We need to be faithful to sow the good seeds that He uses to further His kingdom on this earth. Let God weed out the bad fruit in our lives and then the vines won't get choked out.

Does your vineyard look like a sluggard or a wife of noble character?

> *"I went past the field of a sluggard, past the vineyard of someone who has no sense; thorns had come up everywhere, the ground was covered with weeds, and the stone wall was in ruins."*
> ~ Proverbs 24:30-31

> *"She goes to inspect a field and buys it; with her earnings she plants a vineyard. She is energetic and strong, a hard worker."*
> ~ Proverbs 31:16-17 (NLT)

How do you fertilize your vineyard to help produce good fruit daily?

> Through prayer,
> > reading Scripture,
> > > spending time alone with the gardener,
> > > > praising the gardener, and
> > > > > fellowship with like-minded people.

How can you be sure to produce good fruit?

> *"Remain in me, and I will remain in you.*
> *For a branch cannot produce fruit if it is severed from the vine,*
> *and you cannot be fruitful unless you remain in me.*
> *Yes, I am the vine; you are the branches.*
> *Those who remain in me, and I in them, will produce much fruit.*
> *For apart from me you can do nothing."*
> ~ John 15:4-5 (NLT)

We need to always remain united with Jesus, connected to the true grapevine. We need the power He provides to help sustain us. Our lives will then produce an abundant harvest of good fruit as He works in and through us.

Who chose you to produce lasting fruit?

> *"You didn't choose me. I chose you.*
> *I appointed you to go and produce lasting fruit,*
> *so that the Father will give you whatever you ask for, using my name.*
> *This is my command: Love each other."*
> ~ John 15:16-17 (NLT)

Jesus has chosen you to produce lasting fruit with your life and vineyard. Let the fruit of love reign overall. You will be able to serve the finest wine with the best fruit from your vineyard. Keep harvesting the good fruit in all you do and in who you are for the Lord.

May you be encouraged to…

> remain connected to Jesus, the true vine.
> sow the good seeds.
> let the gardener, God our Father, help till your vineyard.
> serve the finest wine with your life.
> love everyone.

REFLECTION:

What seeds do you need to sow fewer of?
Which seeds do you sow the most?

> *"God blesses those who are merciful, for they will be shown mercy."*
> *~ Matthew 5:7 (NLT)*

30

Be Still

*"Be still and know that I'm with you.
Be still and know I am."*

The words above are from a song entitled "Be Still" by The Fray.[1]

Take time each day to be still
    Get away from the hustle and bustle
        Even if for five minutes
            Spending time basking in God's love and presence.

In our busy, hectic, fast-paced lives, the most important thing we can do each day is to spend a few moments in silence with the Lord. What great advice that is vital to knowing God more intimately and allowing Him to work more powerfully.

Consider Jesus' example,

"But Jesus himself would often slip away to the wilderness and pray."
~ Luke 5:16 (NASB)

"Very early in the morning, while it was still dark, Jesus got up, left the house and went off to a solitary place, where he prayed."
~ Mark 1:35

"It was at this time that he went off to the mountain to pray, and he spent the whole night in prayer to God."
~ Luke 6:12 (NASB)

> *"And he said to them, 'Come away by yourselves*
> *to a desolate place and rest a while.'*
> *For many were coming and going, and they had no leisure even to eat."*
> ~ Mark 6:31 (ESV)

Notice in all these Bible verses, Jesus took time to slip away from people and spend time praying with God, His Father. Throughout Jesus' public ministry, He preached, had compassion on many, and even healed the sick and lame, yet He knew the importance of being still with the Father. If Jesus, being God's only Son, modeled this, all the more we need to apply it to our lives.

Jesus took time to pray, listen, and seek God's will for His life, just like we need to. This is especially evident in one of Jesus' last prayers on this earth to God, His Father,

> *"They went to a place called Gethsemane, and Jesus said to his disciples, 'Sit here while I pray.' He took Peter, James and John along with him, and he began to be deeply distressed and troubled. 'My soul is overwhelmed with sorrow to the point of death,' he said to them. 'Stay here and keep watch.' Going a little farther, he fell to the ground and prayed that if possible the hour might pass from him. 'Abba, Father,' he said, 'everything is possible for you. Take this cup from me. Yet not what I will, but what you will.'"*
> ~ Mark 14:32-36

What a wonderful example Jesus left us. Sure, all we do and all we are is done in His name, but if we are always running, doing things, we will miss God speaking to us in the silence. God reveals Himself in the silence, too.

Our pastor gave us the challenge one day to spend a minute of "FaceTime" with Jesus daily. He said we would be surprised to see what a difference it makes in our lives. True to what he said, I have noticed a big difference in my life when I take fifteen minutes daily to sit in silence in a church and just take time to talk and share with the Lord. There are so many people who need our prayers, and it is a great way to lift them to the Lord and see how He inspires us to minister to someone. Often, I try to follow up right then, whether it is to let someone know I'm praying for them or to check the status of someone I'm praying for.

If you already make time daily for a few moments of alone time to be still with the Lord, let me encourage you to keep it up. That is awesome.

If you struggle with making time to be silent with the Lord, may I challenge you to try five minutes a day? Start with five minutes and you might be surprised that your time might easily turn into fifteen minutes.

Be creative with how you make time to be still by…

>   taking a longer route to the restroom at work.
>   going outside for a quick walk around the building.
>   stopping at your place of worship.
>   turning off the radio in the car.
>   focusing on the Lord while on the bus or train.
>   going to your prayer closet.

Our lives are made so much richer by dwelling on what really matters each day. Personal fellowship with the Lord through praying, listening, and seeking God's will for our lives is most important.

REFLECTION:

What small step can you take to be still with God?
What time of day is best for your prayer time?

> *"Now then, stand still and see this great thing the Lord is about to do before your eyes!"*
> ~ 1 Samuel 12:16

31

Burdens

My eldest son asked me to accompany him in shopping for clothes at a mall. It was a major trip so he could buy appropriate business attire for the launching of his professional career.

After making purchases at the first store, we put the bag in the car. We continued shopping, and gradually the packages accumulated one after another. We never went back to the car because this mall was so huge, and we kept getting further and further away from the car.

We accumulated about eight bags of items, which you wouldn't think would be too heavy, but trust me, they added up in weight and size. The biggest, heaviest one contained two boxes of dress shoes.

Going to a new store meant putting all the bags down to look at items. It was challenging and exhausting. By the end of the shopping trip, I was carrying the packages as weights to help change the position of my hands and arms.

This is what it made me think…

> What if the packages represented burdens that we carry around?

Isn't it so easy to pick up one burden, something that starts to weigh us down and wears on our mind? Maybe even a lie about something we have started to believe? Once we pick up one burden, another one so quickly comes along and we carry that burden. The cycle so easily continues until we are weighed down.

Maybe someone made a negative comment about something you did. You know it's not true, but in your humanity, it starts to weigh you down. A co-worker then comes along and asks you why your deadline isn't met yet. There is another burden to add to your day. You hear about a relative who just found out they have cancer. That sure is a heavy burden that gets added to you.

You try to carry all those burdens alone, but you find it is a heavy load. Just like when at the mall, when my son and I shared the carrying of the packages, the load was made a little easier. Sometimes, it helps to share that burden with another. Maybe that person will say something that helps us see the error of our way in picking up the burden. Sometimes, knowing someone is praying for us helps us get through the day.

What else can we do differently? How about trying to lay down the burden as soon as we start to pick it up? Maybe there is no need to pick it up, especially if it is something that is not that important.

How about following Jesus' example after He was in the desert for 40 days and 40 nights being tempted by Satan? He fought all of Satan's attacks with Scripture, which is the truth that will help us carry the burdens and find rest for ourselves. Talk to God, lay down your burdens at the cross, and watch Him carry them for you. He is right there beside you, helping you.

REFLECTION:

What burden are you carrying that you can lay down at the cross?
Who did you help carry a heavy burden for?

> *"Cast your cares on the Lord and he will sustain you;*
> *He will never let the righteous fall."*
> ~ Psalm 55:22

32

Places of Honor

"Then James and John, the sons of Zebedee, came to him. 'Teacher,' they said, 'we want you to do for us whatever we ask.' 'What do you want me to do for you?' he asked. They replied, 'Let one of us sit at your right and the other at your left in your glory.' 'You don't know what you are asking,' Jesus said. 'Can you drink the cup I drink or be baptized with the baptism I am baptized with?' 'We can,' they answered. Jesus said to them, 'You will drink the cup I drink and be baptized with the baptism I am baptized with, but to sit at my right or left is not for me to grant. These places belong to those for whom they have been prepared.'"
~ Mark 10:35-40

What do we learn about James and John from this story?

> James and John wanted Jesus to do whatever they had in mind for their lives. They wanted a place of honor, prestige, and power to sit next to Jesus in glory.
>
>> How often are we just like James and John, wanting Jesus to do what **we** have in mind for our lives?
>> How often do we let honor, prestige, and power take over in our lives instead of being servants?

How does Jesus respond to their request?

> He says they don't grasp what they are asking. Great suffering is part of being in a position of glory in the kingdom of God. Jesus responds that James and John will share in the cup Jesus drinks

from because of His suffering and death for their salvation. It is a form of baptism. Jesus is not the One to decide who sits to His right and left. God, the Father, who has all authority on earth and in heaven, has already decided who will have the places of honor on Jesus' right and left.

> How often do we want to be in positions of glory in the kingdom of God?
> How often are we willing to suffer to share in the cup of Jesus?

When reading the above Mark passage, I never reflected on who the *"those for whom they have been prepared"* were.

> *"Two others, who were criminals, were led*
> *away to be put to death with him.*
> *And when they came to the place that is called*
> *The Skull, there they crucified him,*
> *and the criminals, one on his right and one on his left."*
> ~ Luke 23:32-33 (ESV)

> *"One of the criminals who were hanged railed at*
> *him, saying, 'Are you not the Christ?*
> *Save yourself and us!' But the other rebuked him, saying, 'Do you not fear God, since you are under the same sentence of condemnation? And we indeed justly, for we are receiving the due reward of our deeds; but this man has done nothing wrong.' And he said, 'Jesus, remember me when you come into your kingdom.' And he said to him, 'Truly, I say to you, today you will be with me in paradise.'"*
> ~ Luke 23:39-43 (ESV)

Who were the two people God had planned to be crucified at Jesus' right and left?

God chose two criminals, two criminals who were justly condemned!

We see that one thief, often known as the bad thief, thinks Jesus is the Savior of the world and wants Him to save Himself and the thieves. His faith is limited by whether Jesus comes down from the cross alive and does the same for them.

The other thief, often known as the good thief, rebukes the bad thief. He realizes that Jesus, who has done no wrong, is being put to death, whereas the two thieves have done wrong and deserve death. The good thief puts his faith and trust in Jesus, asking for salvation. Jesus grants his request.

What could God be teaching us?

Aren't we just like those criminals? We are also justly condemned until we come to repentance. The kingdom of heaven is not for the elite; it is for those who repent and accept Jesus as their Savior. There is no work we can do to earn our salvation; it is God's gift to us. We should not be concerned with worldly honor and power; it is about serving others with a humble heart.

We can place ourselves at the right or left of Jesus at His crucifixion because we, too, are sinners. Are you more like the good or the bad thief?

May you be encouraged to take time to reflect on the goodness of God's love, mercy, and forgiveness, which He extends to us all.

REFLECTION:

Can you think of a time you were like James and John?
Is your heart filled with gratitude like the good thief, recognizing the punishment you deserve that Jesus took upon Himself?

"Let the wicked forsake his way, and the unrighteous man his thoughts; let him return to the Lord, that he may have compassion on him, and to our God, for he will abundantly pardon."
~ Isaiah 55:7 (ESV)

33

Servant of All

This reflection shares the second half of the story from the previous devotional. The other ten disciples became indignant with James and John, who wanted to sit at Jesus' right and left.

> *"Jesus called them together and said, 'You know that those who are regarded as rulers of the Gentiles lord it over them, and their high officials exercise authority over them. Not so with you. Instead, whoever wants to become great among you must be your servant, and whoever wants to be first must be slave of all. For even the Son of Man did not come to be served, but to serve, and to give his life as a ransom for many.'"*
> ~ Mark 10:42-45

What did Jesus say makes one great?
    To be a servant of all.

Who is the greatest servant that ever lived?
    The Son of Man, Jesus.

What is the role of a servant that Jesus' life modeled?
    To put the needs of others first before their own.
    To care about the well-being of others.
    To help set people free from bondage.
    To share God's love rather than dominate in power.

What are some of the ways Jesus served others? Feel free to take a few minutes to read the Scriptures cited below.

Providing wine for the wedding guests. (John 2:1-11)
> Jesus did not want the people hosting the wedding party to be caught in the serious offense of not having enough wine for the feast.

He healed the blind, the lame, and the lepers. (John 9:1-12)
> Jesus noticed those in need as He walked this earth. He often healed people, both spiritually and physically, which reflected God's glory.

Providing food when the crowds were hungry. (Mark 8:1-13)
> Jesus' compassion for the large crowd, who had gathered for three days to listen to Him, was apparent with His concern that if they did not have anything to eat, they would collapse on their walk home.

Extending love and compassion to the adulteress. (John 8:1-11)
> Jesus shared love and compassion with the woman whom the teachers of the law and Pharisees brought to Him. They were trying to condemn her. Because of His love for her, Jesus knew we are all sinners and encouraged this woman to leave her life of sin behind.

What was the ultimate way Jesus served humankind?
> By giving up His life and dying on the cross. He paid the ransom for our sins, despite being sinless.

> A Google search for the definition of servant says: "One that serves others."

> Jesus showed us that serving others is a way of life. Our lives should be characterized by humble and loving service to all those we encounter. We must be willing to serve others without reserve if we want to be great in the kingdom of God.

This quote from the Italian movie, *Life is Beautiful*,[2] gives us more insight into thoughts about serving:

> *"Think of a sunflower, they bow to the sun. But if you see some that are bowed too far down, it means they're dead. You're here serving, you're not a servant. Serving is the supreme art. God is the first of servants. God serves men, but he's not a servant to men."*

When we serve others, we are not doing it as slaves. Instead, our serving should be from a heart of love and compassion. Serving others is a special privilege we have as we strive to emulate the greatest servant. How interesting it is to consider that God is the first servant. Indeed, God lovingly serves us by creating a beautiful world full of nature, animals, and people we can enjoy. He also served us through His plan of redemption.

Take time to reflect on…

> In what ways do you serve others daily?
> Are there special ministries through which you serve others?
> How many times do you want to be served rather than serve?
> Is your heart full of love and compassion as you serve?
> How willing are you to serve others through the ultimate act of love, as Jesus did?

REFLECTION:

Do you serve, even in the little things, with a heart of compassion?
Is the Lord calling you to stretch yourself for a new ministry?

> *"For the Lord will give justice to his people and have compassion on his servants."*
> ~ Psalm 135:14 (NLT)

34

Water Reflections

I was grateful to spend a day in solitude, being still, at Lake Ontario. I spent about eight hours on the shore with my chair, Bible, and notebook. It was a wonderful time of being with the Lord and reflecting.

The shoreline consisted of mounds of stones and some boulders. It was amazing to see the stones and the beauty of their different colors, shapes, and sizes. Most of them appeared to have smooth surfaces from their travels through the water. I was overcome by the beauty of the shoreline and thought about how our lives are so much like those stones. We come in all colors, sizes, and shapes, having quite the journey through the path of life. Sometimes we have smooth times in life and sometimes life becomes jagged. However, we are all beautiful too.

Despite it being October in New York State, I felt prompted to put my feet in the water. Due to the massive number of rocks making it difficult to walk without slipping, I sat down on the rocks, took off my sneakers and socks, and inched my way closer to the water. Immersing my feet in the water made me feel one with the water. Eventually, I stood up. Viewing the vastness of the lake before me, I soaked up the feeling of the water against my feet and ankles as God's presence and peace filled my spirit.

As I sat on the shore of the desolate beach, it was easy to imagine some scenes from Bible stories. I thought of Jesus' baptism in the Jordan River.

> *"In those days Jesus came from Nazareth of Galilee and was baptized by John in the Jordan. And when he came up out of the water, immediately he saw the heavens being torn open and the Spirit*

*descending on him like a dove. And a voice came from heaven,
'You are my beloved Son; with you, I am well pleased.'"*
~ Mark 1:9-11 (ESV)

May we remember at our baptism, we, too, were called "Beloved." We are God's precious children made in His image. May we live knowing that God is well pleased with us.

Looking down the shoreline, I envisioned Jesus calling, "Come, follow me."

"As Jesus was walking beside the Sea of Galilee, he saw two brothers, Simon called Peter and his brother Andrew. They were casting a net into the lake, for they were fishermen. 'Come, follow me,' Jesus said, 'and I will send you out to fish for people.' At once they left their nets and followed him."
~ Matthew 4:18-20

Jesus extends that same invitation to you and me. May we, too, always be open to leaving what we are doing to follow Him and put Him first in our lives.

I thought about Jesus calming the turbulent waters of the sea when a big storm came.

"But soon a fierce storm came up. High waves were breaking into the boat, and it began to fill with water. Jesus was sleeping at the back of the boat with his head on a cushion. The disciples woke him up, shouting, 'Teacher, don't you care that we're going to drown?' When Jesus woke up, he rebuked the wind and said to the waves, 'Silence! Be still!' Suddenly the wind stopped, and there was a great calm."
~ Mark 4:37-39 (NLT)

When the storms come crashing into our lives, Jesus is with us, just as He was with the disciples. Sometimes He will tell the storm to "Be Still" immediately. Sometimes we experience His calmness and peace deep in our hearts despite the storm raging around us.

I thought of the trees that grow near bodies of water.

> *"But they delight in the law of the Lord, meditating on it day and night. They are like trees planted along the riverbank, bearing fruit each season. Their leaves never wither, and they prosper in all they do."*
> ~ Psalm 1:2-3 (NLT)

May our lives be like the trees planted along the riverbanks. May we bear fruit for God every season of our lives, doing His will and sharing His goodness. If we keep the Lord at the forefront of our lives and meditate on His Word, the leaves and fruit of our lives will prosper. We will keep producing the choicest fruit.

Be encouraged to reflect on knowing...

> you are God's beloved.
> Jesus says to you, "Come, follow Me."
> Jesus calms the storms in your life.
> you can produce the choicest fruit.

REFLECTION:

Do you experience God's presence near bodies of water?
What are ways you "Come, follow Me" in your daily life?

> *"Come, all you who are thirsty, come to the waters; and you who have no money, come, buy and eat! Come, buy wine and milk without money and without cost. Why spend money on what is not bread, and your labor on what does not satisfy? Listen, listen to me, and eat what is good, and you will delight in the richest of fare."*
> ~ Isaiah 55:1-2

35

A Rocked World

What are some difficult and unpleasant challenges you have faced? Was the situation hard for a short time and then easier? Can you think of times when your world seemed to be rocked— turned completely upside down?

Was your world rocked due to …

> the death of a loved one?
> cancer or chronic disease diagnosis?
> a marriage that suddenly ended in divorce?
> a child addicted to drugs?

Take a few moments to think about how you typically deal with a rocked world, something that is so devastating and seems like the end of the world.

Do you know some people that seem to handle life so well no matter what they are experiencing or living through? What sets them apart?

> It seems we can either let it overtake and ruin us
> or
> we can try to make the best of a terrible, from
> a worldly view, tragic situation.

When we first hear the devastating news, I think we all agree it is easy to let the situation consume us, maybe even with feelings of hopelessness or helplessness. Hopefully, it won't be long before we come to our senses and try to fight through the negativity that can occur.

What are some key elements to handling a rocked world more successfully?

ALLOW TIME TO GRIEVE.

> Whatever situation you find yourself in, a rocked world equates to needing time to grieve. Realize it is okay to grieve and even struggle/wrestle with the issue at hand. Try to take baby steps to get your feet back on the ground again.

> *"There is a time for everything, and a season for every activity under heaven: a time to weep and a time to laugh, a time to mourn and a time to dance. A time to tear and a time to mend."*
> ~ Ecclesiastes 3:1, 4, 7

REMAIN CONNECTED TO GOD AND YOUR FAITH.

> Go to church services. Ask ministers and other church members to pray for and with you.

> *"Is anyone among you sick? Let them call the elders of the church to pray over them and anoint them with oil in the name of the Lord."*
> ~ James 5:14

SEEK A FEW CHRISTIAN FRIENDS TO REACH OUT TO.

> Those people you know on a more personal level who will stand with you for encouragement and support. They will faithfully pray for you through the crisis and will step in with faith when yours might be faltering.

> *"Two are better than one, because they have a good return for their labor: If either of them falls down, one can help the other up. But pity anyone who falls and has no one to help them him up!"*
> ~ Ecclesiastes 4:9-10

Pray continually for guidance and direction.

> If you find comfort there, go to a church, even an empty one. If seeking the Lord there ministers to you, get down on your knees and share your heart with God.

"Rejoice in hope, be patient in tribulation, be constant in prayer."
~ Romans 12:12 (ESV)

Look for ways God is speaking and leading you.

> Maybe God will use people in your life to say something that is just what you need at the moment. Perhaps it will be something you read or see that will minister to you.

"And the Word became flesh and dwelt among us, and we have seen his glory, glory as of the only Son from the Father, full of grace and truth."
~ John 1:14 (ESV)

Look for God's promises in the Bible.

> Let His words speak and minister to your heart, providing you with courage and strength.

"Have I not commanded you? Be strong and courageous. Do not be afraid; do not be discouraged, for the Lord your God will be with you wherever you go."
~ Joshua 1:9

"And my God will meet all your needs according to the riches of his glory in Christ Jesus."
~ Philippians 4:19

"And we know that in all things God works for the good of those who love him, who have been called according to his purpose."
~ Romans 8:28

I am humbled to share this journey of life with some dear friends who suffer daily from chronic illnesses, immobility, constant pain, and other issues that you might not notice. For many of them, their lives were rocked and turned upside down in the blink of an eye. Yet, as I reflect on them, their situations, and their lives, I realize each of them are a daily inspiration. They live with great faith, love, and positivity, taking one moment, one step at a time. What a wonderful example and way to live.

If you know people whose life is being rocked, be sure to reach out to them and do your part to help them through their situation. Pray with them, encourage them, be there, brighten their day, and allow Christ to work through you.

My prayer for you when your world is rocked is that God may touch you and that deep down in the recesses of your heart you may still know the joy that Jesus brings. May you find comfort and joy from this well-known, beautiful psalm that David wrote, especially when you are living in a rocked world.

"The Lord is my shepherd, I lack nothing. He makes me lie down in green pastures, he leads me beside quiet waters, he refreshes my soul. He guides me along the right paths for his name's sake. Even though I walk through the darkest valley, I will fear no evil, for you are with me; your rod and your staff, they comfort me. You prepare a table before me in the presence of my enemies. You anoint my head with oil; my cup overflows. Surely your goodness and love will follow me all the days of my life, and I will dwell in the house of the Lord forever."
~ Psalm 23:1-6

REFLECTION:

Is there something you can do differently when your world gets rocked? Who can you reach out to help as their world is rocked?

"Your compassion, Lord, is great; preserve my life according to your laws."
~ Psalm 119:156

36

Confess

As a result of Adam and Eve's disobedience with eating from the tree of knowledge in the Garden of Eden, we are all born into sin. It is a rebellion and a rejection of God and all that is good. It is an offense against a holy and righteous God.

> *"When Adam sinned, sin entered the world. Adam's sin brought death, so death spread to everyone, for everyone sinned."*
> ~ Romans 5:12 (NLT)

Once we accept Jesus as our Lord and Savior, we become right with God. This sin no longer has power over our lives as we belong to a holy, righteous God.

> *"God made him who had no sin to be sin for us, so that in him we might become the righteousness of God."*
> ~ 2 Corinthians 5:21

> *"We know that our old sinful selves were crucified with Christ so that sin might lose its power in our lives. We are no longer slaves to sin."*
> ~ Romans 6:6 (NLT)

As humans, we still commit sins. Sins are contrary to the will of God and a turning away from Him. It can be a failure to do what is right or something we should have done.

What did Jesus say are the two greatest commandments?

> *"Jesus replied: 'Love the Lord your God with all your heart and with all your soul and with all your mind.' This is the first and greatest commandment. And the second is like it: 'Love your neighbor as yourself.'"*
> – Matthew 22:37-39

The sins in our lives, I believe, can be measured against these two commandments Jesus gave us.

> *"If we confess our sins, he is faithful and just to forgive us our sins and to cleanse us from all unrighteousness."*
> – 1 John 1:9 (ESV)

If we take time to think about, confess, and truly repent of our sins, God is faithful to forgive us and cleanse us. This passage was powerful for me one day as I was confessing my sins and then went for a walk outside. There was a gentle rain, and I was reminded of God cleansing me in the sea of His forgiveness. A few minutes later, the sun came out, reminding me of Jesus, the Son, redeeming me back to wholeness because of the power of the Resurrection.

> *"For, there is one God and one Mediator who can reconcile God and humanity— the man Christ Jesus. He gave his life to purchase freedom for everyone. This is the message God gave to the world at just the right time."*
> – 1 Timothy 2:5-6 (NLT)

Thanks be to God for sending His only Son, Jesus, to this earth to reconcile us back to God despite our sinfulness. This freedom is available to anyone who believes in Jesus.

It is powerful to consider how God then remembers our sins no more. We truly are set free. In our humanity, we are the ones that find it hard to forget our sins. If God remembers them no longer, we should let them go as well.

*"For I will be merciful toward their iniquities, and
I will remember their sins no more."*
~ Hebrews 8:12 (ESV)

"He has removed our sins as far from us as the east is from the west."
~ Psalm 103:12 (NLT)

May these thoughts inspire you to...

> share with God the ways your actions have failed to love Him and others.
> seek God's forgiveness by confessing your sins.
> praise Jesus for the freedom you have from your sins.
> be joyful, knowing God remembers your sins no more.

Keep striving to move forward, living out the two greatest commandments daily.

REFLECTION:

Do you take time to regularly share and ask God's forgiveness for your sins? Does loving God and others guide your actions and the way you live?

*"To give his people the knowledge of salvation through the
forgiveness of their sins, because of the tender mercy of our God,
by which the rising sun will come to us from heaven."*
~ Luke 1:77-78

37

Do Not Cling

Do you sometimes read or hear a familiar Scripture passage, and suddenly you see something you have never noticed before? I had one of those experiences with this story about Jesus' resurrection.

> *"Mary was standing outside the tomb crying, and as she wept, she stooped and looked in. She saw two white-robed angels, one sitting at the head and the other at the foot of the place where the body of Jesus had been lying. 'Dear woman, why are you crying?' the angels asked her. 'Because they have taken away my Lord,' she replied, 'and I don't know where they have put him.' She turned to leave and saw someone standing there. It was Jesus, but she didn't recognize him. 'Dear woman, why are you crying?' Jesus asked her. 'Who are you looking for?' She thought he was the gardener. 'Sir,' she said, 'if you have taken him away, tell me where you have put him, and I will go and get him.' 'Mary!' Jesus said. She turned to him and cried out, 'Rabboni!' (which is Hebrew for "Teacher"). 'Don't cling to me,' Jesus said, 'for I haven't yet ascended to the Father. But go find my brothers and tell them, "I am ascending to my Father and your Father, to my God and your God." Mary Magdalene found the disciples and told them, 'I have seen the Lord!' Then she gave them his message."*
> ~ John 20:11-18 (NLT)

Mary Magdalene went to the tomb early on the first day of the week while it was still dark. She was prepared to anoint and ready Jesus' body for entombment. Mary was surprised and distraught to see Jesus' body was missing from the tomb. In her desperation to find His body, she was willing to do whatever it took to find Him. Much to her surprise, Jesus, in

His resurrected state, was right in front of her. She recognized Him once He said her name. What a deep love she had for Jesus.

Why was Mary's love for Jesus so deep?

> Jesus cast seven demons out of her. (Luke 8:2) She experienced Jesus' life-changing power in her life.
> Mary Magdalene was a follower of Jesus and helped support His ministry. (Luke 8:3) She wanted to help spread the good news of Jesus to others as well as grow in her relationship with Jesus.
> She was present at the foot of the cross at Jesus' crucifixion. (John 19:25)
> Mary saw where Jesus was laid in the tomb. (Mark 15:47)

The phrase that jumped out at me from the Scripture was Jesus saying, *"Don't cling to me."* Can you see Mary Magdalene's fists clenched, holding on tightly to Jesus' cloak? Mary dearly loved Jesus and did not want to let Him go. Isn't that just like when we lose someone near and dear?

What are some possible reasons Jesus said this to Mary?

Jesus understood Mary was scared and afraid to lose Him again, but…

> It was important for the disciples to know He was alive, just as He foretold. Mary Magdalene, the person Jesus first appeared to, was given the task of sharing the news of His resurrection with the disciples.

> > He knew Mary would still have opportunities to visit with Him before His ascension into heaven.

> > > Death brings a change in relationships with people.

> We can't hold on to the old. We always need to be growing and changing.

>> If we have clenched fists, we can't give or receive anything new.

>>> Jesus knew Mary could not rely solely on His physical presence. Once He ascended, the third person of the Trinity, the Holy Spirit, would be our access.

As you continue to celebrate the Risen Lord in your life, how can you be more like Mary Magdalene with…

> sharing the good news of "I have seen the Lord?"
> recognizing the Holy Spirit's presence in your life?
> unclenching your fists to give and receive new blessings?

Because of Jesus' resurrection and ascension into heaven, we…

> know Jesus calls us by name.
> live in peace, knowing we are never alone. Jesus left us the Holy Spirit.
> know we have the same Father and God that Jesus has.

REFLECTION:

Do you need to unclench your fists with something in your life?
Do you recognize the Holy Spirit's presence leading and guiding you?

> *"Remember, O Lord your compassion and unfailing love,*
> *which you have shown from long ages past."*
> ~ Psalm 25:6 (NLT)

38

Prepare the Way

There are many parallels between John the Baptist and Jesus' lives and what their purposes on this earth were all about.

John's life purpose on earth echoes our own. Let's look at some differences and similarities that surrounded John and Jesus' earliest beginnings. As always, feel free to take a few moments to read the following Scripture references.

THE BIRTH OF JOHN THE BAPTIST FORETOLD. (Based on Luke 1:5-25; 57-66)

Summary:

> Zechariah & Elizabeth were very advanced in age, barren, and desperately wanted a child.
>
> The angel Gabriel appeared to Zechariah on the day he was chosen by lot to go into the temple of the Lord and burn incense.
>
> Gabriel told Zechariah that Elizabeth would bear him a son whose name would be John.
>
> John would bring joy and delight to them, and many would rejoice in his birth.
>
> John would be great in the sight of the Lord.
>
> John would be filled with the Holy Spirit even from birth.

John's ministry would be to make ready a people prepared for the Lord.

Zechariah, because he did not believe what Gabriel had said, could not speak until after John was born and circumcised on the eighth day.

The Birth of Jesus Foretold. (Based on Luke 1:26-38)

Summary:

Mary, a young virgin, was pledged to be married to Joseph.

The angel Gabriel appeared to Mary, telling her she was highly favored and the Lord was with her.

Mary wondered what this meant. Gabriel reassured her not to be afraid as she had found favor with God.

Mary would be with child, a son whose name would be Jesus. Mary wondered how this would happen since she was a virgin.

Gabriel said the Holy Spirit would come upon her with the power of the Most High overshadowing her.

Jesus would be great, being called the Son of the Most High and the Son of God.

God would give Jesus the throne of his father David, so that He would reign over the house of Jacob forever. His kingdom would never end.

Mary trusted him and said she was the Lord's servant and *"may it be to me as you have said."*

Similarities:

The angel Gabriel appeared to both Zechariah and Mary.

The Holy Spirit was at work in both John and Jesus, even while in the womb.

Elizabeth and Mary would both have special babies, overlapping in their pregnancies.

Differences:

Elizabeth was old; Mary was young.

Zechariah did not trust God to give them a baby; Mary accepted that God would do what Gabriel foretold.

John was to point everyone to Jesus; Jesus is the Savior of the world. John the Baptist is recorded as only saying a few words, yet his role was to point everyone to Jesus. What few things did he say that pointed everyone to Jesus?

> *"I baptize with water those who repent of their sins and turn to God. But someone is coming soon who is greater than I am— so much greater that I'm not worthy even to be his slave and carry his sandals. He will baptize you with the Holy Spirit and with fire."*
> *~ Matthew 3:11 (NLT)*

From the beginning of John's ministry, he knew that there was one coming greater than he was.

John the Baptist announces twice that Jesus is the "Lamb of God."

> *"The next day John saw Jesus coming toward him and said, 'Look! The Lamb of God who takes away the sin of the world!'"*
> *~ John 1:29 (NLT)*

> *"The following day John was again standing with two
> of his disciples. As Jesus walked by, John looked at him
> and declared, 'Look! There is the Lamb of God!'"*
> ~ John 1:35-36 (NLT)

John recognized that Jesus was the Lamb of God, the one who would be the sacrifice to atone for the sins of the world.

> *"He (Jesus) must become greater and greater,
> and I must become less and less."*
> ~ John 3:30 (NLT)

John realized the importance of Jesus shining through in our lives; more of Him, less of us.

> *"And this is the testimony of John, when the Jews sent priests and
> Levites from Jerusalem to ask him, 'Who are you?' He confessed,
> and did not deny, but confessed, 'I am not the Christ.'"*
> ~ John 1:19-20 (ESV)

John was honest, stating he was not the Christ, even encouraging his followers to follow Jesus, not him. That act embraces humility and shows John was not prideful.

Here are some similarities between the public ministries of John and Jesus:

BOTH STARTED THEIR PUBLIC MINISTRIES PREACHING REPENTANCE.

John:
> *"In those days John the Baptist came to the Judean wilderness
> and began preaching. His message was, 'Repent of your sins
> and turn to God, for the Kingdom of Heaven is near.'"*
> ~ Matthew 3:1-2 (NLT)

Jesus:

> "From then on Jesus began to preach, 'Repent of your sins and turn to God, for the Kingdom of Heaven is near.'"
> ~ Matthew 4:17 (NLT)

BOTH ENCOURAGED PEOPLE TO SHARE WITH OTHERS.

John:

> "John replied, 'If you have two shirts, give one to the poor. If you have food, share it with those who are hungry.'"
> ~ Luke 3:11 (NLT)

Jesus:

> "Jesus told him, 'If you want to be perfect, go and sell all your possessions and give the money to the poor, and you will have treasure in heaven. Then come, follow me.'"
> ~ Matthew 19:21 (NLT)

BOTH WERE ARRESTED UNJUSTLY.

John:

> "Now Herod had arrested John and bound him and put him in prison because of Herodias, his brother Philip's wife, for John had been saying to him: 'It is not lawful for you to have her.'"
> ~ Matthew 14:3-4

Jesus:

> "So they arrested him and led him to the high priest's home. And Peter followed at a distance."
> ~ Luke 22:54 (NLT)

BOTH SUFFERED TERRIBLE DEATHS.

John:
> *"But at a birthday party for Herod, Herodias's daughter performed a dance that greatly pleased him, so he promised with a vow to give her anything she wanted. At her mother's urging, the girl said, 'I want the head of John the Baptist on a tray!' Then the king regretted what he had said; but because of the vow he had made in front of his guests, he issued the necessary orders. So John was beheaded in the prison, and his head was brought on a tray and given to the girl, who took it to her mother."*
> ~ Matthew 14:6-11 (NLT)

Jesus:
> *"But the mob shouted louder and louder, demanding that Jesus be crucified, and their voices prevailed. So Pilate sentenced Jesus to die as they demanded."*
> ~ Luke 23:23-24 (NLT)

While thinking about John the Baptist's life purpose, take time to reflect on your own life purpose…

> How is God calling you to prepare the way of the Lord?
> How are you pointing others to Jesus?
> How are you glorifying Him?
> Have you repented of your sins and turned to God?
> Do you recognize the Lamb of God in your life and point others to Him?
> Do you ask God to help you decrease and have Christ increase in you?
> Do you keep in mind that you are **not** Christ, which lifts a weight off your shoulders?

Remember…

> to look for the angels that God sends.
> to let the Holy Spirit work in and through you.
> that God can accomplish the impossible in both the young and the old.
> that God's divine will prevails.
> to be attentive to the Spirit's guidance.
> to trust the Lord in all circumstances.

Allow God to fulfill His life purpose for your life.

REFLECTION:

How is God calling you to prepare the way of the Lord?
How are you like John the Baptist in sharing Christ?

> *"The Lord will fulfill his purpose for me; your steadfast love, O Lord, endures forever. Do not forsake the work of your hands."*
> ~ Psalm 138:8 (ESV)

39

Agony of Suffering

Does it bring you comfort to realize Mary, the mother of Jesus, understands what it is like to watch a loved one suffer and endure trials in this life? Her heart must have broken seeing Jesus beaten, scourged, and nailed to a cross. Mary watched first-hand the agony of suffering Jesus endured for your sins and mine.

In thinking about Mary, it brought to mind many I know who are experiencing the agony of suffering with their children. They are watching them deal with cancer treatments, mental illness, making life choices, and heart issues at a young age. We all have people we know dealing with the agony of suffering.

> *"Standing near the cross were Jesus' mother, and his mother's sister, Mary (the wife of Clopas), and Mary Magdalene. When Jesus saw his mother standing there beside the disciple he loved, he said to her, 'Dear woman, here is your son.' And he said to this disciple, 'Here is your mother.' And from then on this disciple took her into his home."*
> ~ John 19:25-27 (NLT)

Jesus, close to death as He was hanging on the cross, acknowledged His mother and the agony she experienced in watching her Son suffer. Jesus assured Mary she was not alone, and John, the beloved disciple, was given the responsibility of taking care of Mary. Mary and John are now "family." Because of Jesus, we are part of this family as well.

Why did Jesus call Mary *"Dear woman"* in the above Scripture? There is one other place in Scripture when Jesus did this.

> *"On the third day a wedding took place at Cana in Galilee. Jesus' mother was there, and Jesus and his disciples had also been invited to the wedding. When the wine was gone, Jesus' mother said to him, 'They have no more wine.' 'Woman, why do you involve me?' Jesus replied. 'My hour has not yet come.' His mother said to the servants, 'Do whatever he tells you.'"*
> ~ John 2:1-5

In both Scriptures, Jesus may have addressed Mary as "*woman*" rather than "mother" to emphasize that He was the Savior of the world for her and all of us. He was being obedient to God, following God's timetable. Jesus did not want Mary, as His mother, to watch her Son endure the agony of suffering, but rather to see the glory of Jesus following God's will.

Jesus is speaking to us as well with these passages.

Be assured and encouraged, knowing…

> Jesus sees us in our agony and knows what it is like to suffer greatly.
> Mary understands the agony of suffering our hearts experience when our loved ones endure hardships.
> God provides "family" in our lives to come alongside us.
> God should be glorified, even in our agony of suffering.

How can we be "family" to those suffering?
> Lift people and situations to the Lord through prayer.
> Prepare and share a meal.
> Send an encouraging note or text.
> Assist with a project as needed.

I encourage you to remember that even in our agony we…

> are understood.
> are never alone.
> have "family."
> should glorify God.

REFLECTION:

When your heart is breaking like Mary's, who else, other than Jesus, can you share it with?
What can you do to encourage someone who is suffering?

"Mercy to the needy is a loan to God and God pays back those loans in full."
~ Proverbs 19:17 (MSG)

40

Tree of Love

Recently, I received an unexpected and unique treasure from a friend. He was cutting wood at his camp when he saw this masterpiece.

He thought of me because he knows God puts hearts in my path daily. The hearts are reminders of God's great love for me, and to remind me to love others with His agape love.

This masterpiece was formed when two lilac trees grew together. Each tree "happened" to have part of the design that formed a perfect heart shape on the inside grain when the two trees became one.

> How did God make that happen?
> How did God make both sides of the heart with threads of purple embedded in them?
> How did God make the outside bark of the two trees also form a heart?

I believe there is a parallel with our lives. What if our life and God were symbolic of the two trees?

When we recognize our need for God, our life becomes united with His. Our hearts then becomes one with God, and we are made whole. Our lives reflect threads of goodness from God's life.

> *"But whoever is united with the Lord is one with him in spirit."*
> ~ 1 Corinthians 6:17

I am in awe of God's display of His love for us even through a piece of wood. God is the creator of everything on this earth. His presence is exalted in and through all of nature. God's love is planted in all things!

Reflecting on the beauty of this wood made me delve into Scripture to see what lessons the trees can teach us.

> *"The Lord God made all sorts of trees grow up from the ground— trees that were beautiful and that produced delicious fruit. In the middle of the garden he placed the tree of life and the tree of the knowledge of good and evil."*
> ~ Genesis 2:9 (NLT)

May our lives be like the most beautiful trees because of the delicious fruit that comes from the love of God reflected through us. May we always keep the tree of life at the center of our lives as we seek to live righteously.

> *"Blessed is the man who trusts in the Lord, whose trust is the Lord. He is like a tree planted by water, that sends out its roots by the stream, and does not fear when heat comes, for its leaves remain green, and is not anxious in the year of drought, for it does not cease to bear fruit."*
> ~ Jeremiah 17:7-8 (ESV)

May we trust the Lord in all circumstances, bearing fruit at all times. May our lives be planted firmly in God, with our roots continually growing and spreading, as God provides us with living water.

> *"Let the trees of the forest sing for joy before the Lord,*
> *for he is coming to judge the earth."*
> *~ 1 Chronicles 16:33 (NLT)*

May we sing for joy before the Lord, as the trees of the forest do, because of His love and goodness for all He has done. We know His righteousness covers the multitude of our sins.

I believe the greatest lesson we can reflect on from the tree is this:

> *"Just as Moses lifted up the snake in the wilderness, so the Son of Man must be lifted up, that everyone who believes may have eternal life in him. For God so loved the world that he gave his one and only Son, that whoever believes in him shall not perish but have eternal life."*
> *~ John 3:14-16*

In the Old Testament, the Lord told Moses to make a bronze serpent and put it on a pole. When someone bitten by a snake looked up at the bronze snake, they would live rather than die (Numbers 21:4-9). So it is with all who look at Jesus lifted on the cross and believes in Him. They will live for all eternity. We have eternal life because Jesus died on the wood of a tree, a tree of love.

May you take a few minutes to reflect upon and give thanks to God for the tree of life He provides in your life.

I encourage you to…

    keep the tree of love at the center of your life.

be like the tree planted near the water, whose roots grow and spread further as you put your trust in God.

sing for joy because of God's goodness in your life.

share your heartfelt gratitude to God for sending Jesus, who died on the tree of love for you personally.

"Let your roots grow down into him, and let your lives be built on him. Then your faith will grow strong in the truth you were taught, and you will overflow with thankfulness."
~ Colossians 2:7 (NLT)

41

Boast In Weakness

A Scripture I have heard many times before took on new meaning for me. It was the night before the launch of my second book, *God's Love Illuminated*. I felt at peace all week after my pastor prayed over me. Well, peace lasted until the night before the launch, when I lay awake for a long time. To calm my spirit, I began reading email devotions.

God used a Proverbs 31 devotion entitled *"You Don't Have to Be Amazing"* to minister to me. It featured the following Scripture passage and, in the thoughts the writer was sharing, the word "boast" was italicized and jumped out at me.

> *"But he said to me, 'My grace is sufficient for you, for my power is made perfect in weakness.' Therefore I will boast all the more gladly of my weaknesses, so that the power of Christ may rest upon me."*
> ~ 2 Corinthians 12:9 (ESV)

I will
> **boast**
>> of my weaknesses...

What a powerful thought!

If we back up a few verses to better understand the context of this passage, Paul writes:

> *"So to keep me from becoming conceited because of the surpassing greatness of the revelations, a thorn was given me in the flesh, a messenger*

of Satan to harass me, to keep me from becoming conceited. Three times I pleaded with the Lord about this, that it should leave me."
~ 2 Corinthians 12:7-8 (ESV)

We know from these passages that Paul experienced some type of thorn in his flesh, though Scripture does not reveal what it was. Maybe it was some physical ailment, or someone made his life miserable, or there was some sin in his life he just could not overcome.

Paul came to terms with the fact that it was not the Lord's will to remove this thorn in his life. He knew if the Lord allowed the affliction to be removed, he would be proud of himself, thinking it was his power, not the Lord's. With Paul having to deal with the thorn, God's divine power would shine through. God's grace, His divine power, is much greater than our human power. Paul knew he could boast in his weakness to show the power of God's grace.

> *"My **grace** is sufficient for you,*
> *for my **power***
> *is made perfect in **weakness**."*

The same truth applies to our lives. In my situation, admitting to God my weakness in public speaking, I prayed that His grace and power would shine through me so I could boast in His goodness. In my own power, I was deficient, but with His grace filling me, I would have victory.

As I was setting things up for the book launch, waiting for people to arrive, I asked a friend to pray over me for good measure. I can honestly say I felt the Holy Spirit's presence empowering me to speak clearly and slowly as I shared my heart about the book. Yes, I can boast of God's goodness by giving me the grace to be confident in my sharing. What a wonderful God we serve.

May you be encouraged to remember…

> God's grace is greater than your weakness.
> to boast of God's power working in you.
> God's power gives you the ability to do His will in your life.

REFLECTION:

What has God given you the strength to do that you thought you couldn't? Which Scripture verse one day spoke to you differently?

> *"For the sake of Christ, then, I am content with*
> *weaknesses, insults, hardships, persecutions, and calamities.*
> *For when I am weak, then I am strong."*
> ~ 2 Corinthians 12:10 (ESV)

42

Living Like the End

Would you live life any differently if you knew with certainty that you had one week left on this earth? Would that knowledge have any impact on what you were doing?

Truthfully, it is a thought that recently occurred to me after learning of the passing of a high school classmate, as well as a friend's brother, who was given a few months to live. My friend was able to spend quality time with her brother and his family in the last six weeks of his life and was with him when he passed.

It made me ponder the life of Jesus.

> Did He know when His hour was coming?
> At what point did He know for sure?
> What did Jesus spend His last days doing?
> Did He give us examples we can model too?

John gives us a few clues into Jesus' knowledge of His impending death. Shortly after Jesus' triumphal entry into Jerusalem on Sunday before the Passover Festival,

> *"Jesus replied, 'The hour has come for the Son of Man to be glorified.'"*
> ~ John 12:23

Jesus knew the end was drawing near with the way things were lining up in His life.

On Thursday, just prior to the celebration of the Passover Festival, we see Jesus knew the time was rapidly approaching.

> *"It was just before the Passover Festival.*
> *Jesus knew that the hour had come for him to*
> *leave this world and go to the Father.*
> *Having loved his own who were in the world,*
> *he loved them to the end."*
> ~ John 13:1

What exactly was Jesus doing during the last week of His earthly life? Are they the things you would be doing too?

His last week was spent:
- teaching
- serving
- praying

Each day from Jesus' triumphal entry to Jerusalem to the time of Passover (Sunday – Thursday), Jesus could be found teaching in the temple during the day. He was praying to God at the Mount of Olives each evening.

> *"Each day Jesus was teaching at the temple, and each evening he went*
> *out to spend the night on the hill called the Mount of Olives, and all*
> *the people came early in the morning to hear him at the temple."*
> ~ Luke 21:37-38

On the day of Jesus' triumphal entry into Jerusalem, Jesus wept for the city of Jerusalem. How He longed for the Jewish people to repent from their ways and recognize that He was the Savior of the world.

> *"As he approached Jerusalem and saw the city, he wept over it and said, '…They will not leave one stone on another, because you did not recognize the time of God's coming to you.'"*
> ~ Luke 19:41-42; 44

Because of prayer's importance, Jesus was trying to have the temple area restored as a place of prayer.

> *"When Jesus entered the temple courts, he began to drive out those who were selling. 'It is written,' he said to them, 'My house will be a house of prayer, but you have made it a den of robbers.'"*
> ~ Luke 19:45-46

At Thursday's Passover Festival, Jesus spent His Last Supper with His closest friends, showing the importance of serving others. He modeled serving through His washing the disciples' feet and by sharing His body and blood with His disciples.

> *"Jesus knew that the Father had put all things under his power, and that he had come from God and was returning to God; so he got up from the meal, took off his outer clothing, and wrapped a towel around his waist. After that, he poured water into a basin and began to wash his disciples' feet, drying them with the towel that was wrapped around him."*
> ~ John 13:3-5

> *"While they were eating, Jesus took bread, and when he had given thanks, he broke it and gave it to his disciples, saying, 'Take it; this is my body.' Then he took a cup, and when he had given thanks, he gave it to them, and they all drank from it. 'This is my blood of the covenant, which is poured out for many,' he said to them."*
> ~ Mark 14:22-24

Jesus prayed for Simon, whom He knew would betray Him.

> "Simon, Simon, Satan has asked to sift you as wheat. But I have prayed for you, Simon, that your faith may not fail. And when you have turned back, strengthen your brothers."
> ~ Luke 22:31-32

Jesus prayed one last time to see if God would take away His cup of suffering.

> "Jesus went out as usual to the Mount of Olives, and his disciples followed him. 'Father if you are willing, take this cup from me; yet not my will, but yours be done.'"
> ~ Luke 22:39; 42

Jesus prayed for Himself, for His disciples, and for all believers.

> "…Father, the time has come. Glorify your Son, that your Son may glorify you."
> ~ John 17:1

> "I pray for them. I am not praying for the world, but for those you have given me, for they are yours."
> ~ John 17:9

> "My prayer is not for them alone. I pray also for those who will believe in me through their message."
> ~ John 17:20

The three main things Jesus did in the last week on earth, aren't they really things He did each and every day of His life, especially in His public ministry? I would also add many miracles and healings.

What a great example Jesus modeled for us to emulate.

How should we live each day?

Teaching– tell others about Jesus and the salvation He grants us through His death on the cross. Share the ways you see Him working in your life to encourage others.

Serving– by looking for ways to serve the Body of Christ, which includes everyone we meet. Use the gifts and talents that God has given you to serve others.

Praying– remembering those in need, our friends, and even more so, our enemies. We can continually pray, and our lives can be an offering of prayer to God.

So let me ask you once more…

> Would you live life any differently if you knew with certainty that you had one week left on this earth?
> Would that knowledge have any impact on what you were doing?
> Did your original answer change or not?

May these thoughts encourage you to live each day to the fullest, modeling the examples Jesus shared with us.

Be a disciple of Jesus by teaching, serving, and praying. Spread the Word of God. You are an important part of the kingdom of God.

REFLECTION:

Do you need to spend a little more time teaching, serving, or praying to be more like Jesus?
In what ways are you serving others?

> *"I will strengthen Judah and save Israel; I will restore them because of my compassion. It will be as though I had never rejected them, for I am the Lord their God, who will hear their cries."*
> ~ Zechariah 10:6 (NLT)

43

Second Chances

As I was watching a season of *American Idol*, the theme of second chances resonated with me. The show highlighted some contestants who came back, providing a second chance at making it to Hollywood. Some previously made it to Hollywood, but their dream came to an end, and they wanted another chance.

Second chances made me think about our relationship with the Lord. It is good to reflect on how God gives us second chances.

What is the most important time in your life when God provided a second chance for you? It was the point in your life when you were ready to accept Him into your life and heart. At that moment, He forgave you of all your sins. That is the ultimate reason why Jesus came to this earth: to give us a second chance to live with Him forever in heaven.

It would be nice if once we accepted Jesus, we did not sin anymore, but Jesus is the only person who walked this earth who did not sin. That is because He is also God.

> *"But you know that he appeared so that he might*
> *take away our sins. And in him is no sin."*
> *- 1 John 3:5*

As much as I think we humans strive to be "perfect" and not sin, that is not possible on this earth. It seems that, because of this, every day we are given second chances.

Maybe second chances can be viewed in two ways…

>one being where we have wronged someone in some way.
>one being opportunities where God's intervening is evident.

What second chances has God given you when you wronged someone?

Maybe it was the time you…

>caught yourself gossiping about a co-worker.
>caught yourself cursing at the driver who cut you off.
>lost your temper with your child or spouse.
>were speeding because you were running late.
>ignored the homeless person on the street.

These are times when our second chances are opportunities to ask the Lord and maybe another person for forgiveness. We can start each day anew with a renewed love for the Lord and others. In doing this, we can once again experience the fullness of the blessings of the Lord.

What second chance has God given where you have seen Him intervene in your life?

Maybe…

>a chance to renew a strained family relationship.
>you were healed of a health issue.
>freedom from an addiction.
>to pursue a new career path where God is called you.
>protection from a disaster that you saw coming.

These second chances are pure blessings from the Lord to help increase our faith and show the Creator's mighty power.

May we strive to live as Jesus loving and serving all we meet and giving it our all, just like the contestants on *American Idol*.

May we always be thankful to the Lord for all the second chances He provides, just like the contestants on *American Idol*, who were so thankful for their second chances.

May we always strive to live in peace and honor the Lord in all that we do.

REFLECTION:

What is a second chance you received from God?
Whom have you blessed with a second chance?

> *"To the Lord our God belong compassion and forgiveness, because we have rebelled against him."*
> ~ Daniel 9:9 (NASB)

44

Heart of Stone

My latest treasures from God on my daily prayer walks have been physical hearts made of stones or blacktop. God reveals His great love for me with the heart theme that has been ongoing since December 2020. I am in awe of Him and how He directs my steps to find these reminders of His love. Different thoughts will come to mind when I discover one of these hearts.

"Walk in love," I thought as I picked up the first stone. The second stone made me smile, as it could be the "big brother" of the first one. When I found the third heart stone, I thought how special it was that I now had the Trinity— the Father, the Son, and the Holy Spirit. Yes, they all walk with me.

When I saw the fourth stone, I was overwhelmed with God's love. How could this stone, with such a perfectly etched heart image with the heart facing up, be in my path? It was by a fence near my church. It is unique as there is a slit and a fossil imprint on the top right. How did this stone get there all of a sudden? How old is it? It is a path I walk every day and is not near any body of water.

Seeing this fourth stone, the phrase "heart of stone" from the Bible came to mind. I immediately prayed for the Lord to soften my heart and for those I know who do not believe in God.

"I will give them an undivided heart and put a new spirit in them; I will remove from them their heart of stone and give them a heart of flesh. Then they will follow my decrees and be careful to keep my laws. They will be my people, and I will be their God."
~ Ezekiel 11:19-20

"I will give you a new heart and put a new spirit in you; I will remove from you your heart of stone and give you a heart of flesh. And I will put my Spirit in you and move you to follow my decrees and be careful to keep my laws. Then you will live in the land I gave your ancestors; you will be my people, and I will be your God."
~ Ezekiel 36:26-28

Both sets of these verses share what God is speaking about the promised return of Israel. Being driven from Jerusalem, the Israelites became exiles. God became their sanctuary, present with them. They were scattered among different nations, but God promised to bring them back to their land. The people would return to God after relinquishing the idols they were worshipping. I believe this message was one of great importance and encouragement to the Israelites since God repeated the same message twice. Notice in the second set, God makes it more personal for them by saying, *"you."*

"I will remove from you your heart of stone and give you a heart of flesh."

What is a heart of stone versus a heart of flesh?

> *"Then in the morning, when Nabal was sober,*
> *his wife told him all these things,*
> *and his heart failed him and he became like a stone."*
> *~ 1 Samuel 25:37*

A heart of stone is a heart that is spiritually dead.

> No love for God.
> Insensitive to God working.
> Sin is rampant.
> Moral insensitivity.
> Blind to the needs of others.

> *"I will give them hearts that recognize me as the Lord.*
> *They will be my people, and I will be their God,*
> *for they will return to me wholeheartedly."*
> *~ Jeremiah 24:7 (NLT)*

A heart of flesh is a heart that is spiritually alive.

> Recognize God in their lives.
> Despite being aware of their flaws, they repent.
> Inner spiritual and moral transformation takes place.
> Single-minded commitment to the Lord and to His will.
> A softened, teachable heart.
> Following the Holy Spirit's leading.
> Sees the needs of others and acts on them.

May you be encouraged to…

> pursue God with an undivided heart.
> ask God to remove the areas of your heart made of stone.
> work on increasing the areas of your heart of flesh.
> seek God's new spirit of transformation.
> know God is with you and helping you.
> follow God's laws, especially the greatest law of love.
> pray for your own heart.
> pray for the hearts of others.

REFLECTION:

Do you pray for those you know who have hearts of stone?
Is your heart more flesh or stone?

> *"Therefore God has mercy on whom he wants to have mercy, and he hardens whom he wants to harden."*
> ~ Romans 9:18

Section 3

GOD'S COMPASSION ILLUMINATED IN ACTIVITIES

"This is what the Lord Almighty said:
'Administer true justice; show mercy and compassion to one another.'"
~ Zechariah 7:9

The way Jesus treated others and the activities He engaged in all brought glory to God as He followed God's way. Striving to follow Jesus' example through the activities we minister in is a great goal to have.

God and Jesus modeled compassion for us, and we need to put our compassion into action. It is a natural way for us to share God's love and to give glory to Him. Jesus' greatest act of compassion was dying on the cross to set us free. Be encouraged to put God's compassion into action by the way you live.

God's compassion illuminated in activities.

"It is not enough to be compassionate, we must act."
~ Dalia Lama

45

The Littlest Details

God cares about the littlest details of our lives. It was a thought that came to mind when I found two tiny heart-shaped stones on the same day while walking and praying.

> *"What is the price of two sparrows— one copper coin? But not a single sparrow can fall to the ground without your Father knowing it. And the very hairs on your head are all numbered. So don't be afraid; you are more valuable to God than a whole flock of sparrows."*
> ~ Matthew 10:29-31 (NLT)

Jesus spoke about one of the smallest of birds to show how God is even concerned about them. God knows and cares when one of the sparrows falls to the ground. I experience God's great love when I consider He knows the very number of hairs on my head. He cares about me and every detail of my life. What a great God.

How often do we pray to God only about the big things in our lives?

Don't we usually pray when we are making a career decision, going through a major crisis, or asking God to heal someone?

Every aspect of our life is so valuable to God, and He cares so much about the littlest detail. God proved this truth to me one day, as I was feeling sad and praying for a friend with a brain tumor. God gave me a heart stone that I saw on the ground to remind me of His love and care.

How often do we share with God when we need a little strength to make it through a day when we only slept few hours the night before?

Do we let God know how we are feeling when someone betrays us or says something demeaning to us?

Be encouraged to remember…

> God is your Father.
> God has great love for you.
> you are so valuable to God.
> God cares about the littlest details in your life.
> to share even the littlest details with God.

Take time each day to share with God…

> the person in your heart you empathize with for the struggle they are going through.
> when you are feeling lonely and want a sign of His presence.
> when you are sad your plans did not work out.
> when you lose something that has sentimental value.

God cares about all the details of your life ~ both the biggest and the littlest details.

REFLECTION:

What are some little details you can share with God today?
Do you talk to God, who is your Father, as you do to a friend?

> *"I tell you the truth, until heaven and earth disappear, not even the smallest detail of God's law will disappear until its purpose is achieved."*
> ~ Matthew 5:18 (NLT)

46

An Invitation

It was a beautiful sunny fall afternoon as I headed for a long-awaited weekend retreat at one of my holy places. After a two-year break from a weekend retreat because of the pandemic, it was special to be back.

Toward the end of my drive, I started playing random songs from the 1,019 songs on a flash drive in my car. The final song as I pulled into the retreat center was "Be Still."

It had been many months since I played that song. I took it as an invitation from the Lord to indeed "Be Still" and experience Him during the weekend in the quiet. I felt led to eat my meals with just the Lord and His Word in a quiet room rather than in the dining room with others.

After getting settled in my room, I went outside for the hour before the retreat started. I noticed the stillness of the lake. It was peaceful and perfectly calm. There was a fishing boat still in the water. At the forest-like area in the distance, I could see two then three deer, calmly grazing, and looking around. There were the peaceful sounds of some birds and peepers.

The horizon was turning beautiful colors— a blend of orange and purple. The sun was glowing as it was setting. It seemed like all of nature was showing me the example of "Be Still." I soaked up the beauty as my soul, too, was still. God graced me with a purple cross in the sky with the cloud formation over the lake.

Observing nature in its stillness reminded me of the peace deep in my heart as I communed with the Lord. His presence brings that peace into our lives. I thought of these Bible verses.

> *"Be still in the presence of the Lord, and wait patiently for him to act…"*
> *~ Psalm 37:7 (NLT)*

> *"Be still, and know that I am God. I will be exalted among the nations, I will be exalted in the earth!"*
> *~ Psalm 46:10 (ESV)*

When we accept the invitation to be still with the Lord, we are assured He will work on our behalf. He works everything out for our good. In stillness, we know in our hearts that God is above all. Why should we fear? God is exalted in all the earth.

On the second day of the retreat, one speaker said, "I put on the table the lyrics to a song that I find so meaningful." He thought the message of the song fit perfectly with one of the previous talks of the weekend. The song touched his spirit. I think my jaw dropped when he said the song was "Be Still," the exact song that was playing in my car as I drove into the retreat center! I was in awe of God, confirming the invitation to be still. Out of the 1,019 songs in my car, how could this speaker mention the same song?

What are other invitations God extends to us?

> *"For God so loved the world that he gave his one and only Son, that whoever believes in him shall not perish but have eternal life."*
> *~ John 3:16*

When we accept the invitation to believe in Jesus, we have eternal life, which is the best gift we can have.

> *"Seek the Lord and his strength; seek his presence continually!"*
> *~ 1 Chronicles 16:11 (ESV)*

When we accept the invitation of seeking the Lord, we possess His strength within us. We are assured of His presence with us always. He never leaves or forsakes us.

> *"Trust in the Lord with all your heart, and do not lean on your own understanding."*
> *~ Proverbs 3:5 (ESV)*

When we accept the invitation to trust the Lord with all we have, we lean into God's understanding. His ways are best, and they are not always our way. We don't have to figure everything out.

> *"Then Jesus said, 'Come to me, all of you who are weary and carry heavy burdens, and I will give you rest.'"*
> *~ Matthew 11:28 (NLT)*

When we accept the invitation to come to Jesus when weary and heavy-laden, we find rest in Him. When life seems too difficult for us, we need to leave it in God's capable hands.

May you be encouraged to reflect on the invitations God has extended to you.

Be encouraged to be still…

> to believe in Jesus.
> to seek the Lord and His presence continually.
> to trust the Lord.
> and when you are weary,
> go to Jesus for rest.

REFLECTION:

Where can you go to be still with God today?
What is God inviting you to today?

*"The Lord is my shepherd, I lack nothing. He
makes me lie down in green pastures,
he leads me beside quiet waters, he refreshes my soul.
He guides me along the right paths for his name's sake."*
- Psalm 23:1-3

47

Divine Encounters

God is so amazing with how He works events out in our lives with His divine encounters. One day at my newest holy place in nature, I heard a single bird singing. When I looked up, I saw it was a cardinal.

A few minutes earlier, I was praying for a family who lost their 18-year-old son. Suddenly the thought of one of my grandmothers came to my mind. I knew she died in June and as I looked up the date, I discovered the anniversary date of her death was the very next day, 31 years earlier. To add to that divine encounter of seeing the cardinal, the next day, I shared the story with one of my aunts (one of my grandmother's daughters). She, too, saw a cardinal on her deck the same day, and thought of my grandmother.

Another day, I was disappointed about something that did not work out like I was hoping. I knew it was the perfect time to talk with the Lord at my usual holy place in nature. When I went to my car to drop off my Bible before taking a quick walk, a car drove into a parking spot near me.

A woman rolled down the window and asked if the church was open. I explained that services wouldn't start until Sunday. She rolled up her window, stayed there, and seemed to be praying. I stood next to my car for a few minutes and felt I should ask her if I could pray with her. She seemed distressed and, knowing she wanted to go into church, maybe she needed some prayer.

When I asked, right away she said, "Sure!" I prayed for her, not knowing what specifically she needed. Much to my amazement, when I finished praying, she prayed for me. I got chills as she prayed. Praying out loud with a stranger is so **not** me, but I am thankful for the Spirit's guidance and that I was obedient.

We then proceeded to talk more, learning some about each other's stories. She worked nearby and said God told her to stop by the church; a church she had never stopped at before. At first, she was reluctant, but God won out, as she was obedient to that voice. Two strangers ended up talking about the Lord, life, and faith for at least 30 minutes because of a divine encounter orchestrated by God and obedience to the Spirit.

God provided another divine encounter with a fellow parishioner one day. As I pulled into the parking lot of my holy place, later than usual, I noticed a lone car there and saw a parishioner leaving the church. The extra "God moment" was that he was hoping to be able to share a few God stories with me in person, rather than via email. Quite in God-like fashion, one story was about the theme of obedience. God provided the opportunity for that divine encounter to bless and encourage each other's faith.

May these thoughts encourage you to see what divine encounters God puts in your path and be obedient to the voice you hear leading you. God is so gracious and kind, offering us ways to praise Him and see His goodness.

REFLECTION:

What is the last divine orchestration you noticed in your life?
Do you try to be obedient to the Lord?

"This is what the Lord Almighty said:
'Administer true justice; show mercy and compassion to one another.'"
~ Zechariah 7:9

48

Airports

Airports are a fascinating place where I get sentimental and reflective as I watch people. Have you taken time to observe the people gathered in an airport before loved ones go through security? I did this the day I was dropping my daughter off for her first lone flight.

For those who were departing, I could sense the bitter-sweet emotions. Bear hugs were exchanged for some people, "I'll miss you," and well wishes were extended; even a few tears or looks of sadness could be seen. One couple was saying goodbye to their Chinese foreign exchange student who was ready to travel home, halfway across the world.

You could tell those people who were awaiting the arrival of loved ones. Their faces displayed looks of anticipation and excitement, watching closely to see their special someone walking down the hallway.

And, if you're like me, the day I was waiting to see my mom return, you might be standing on your tiptoes, stretching from side to side, trying to see over the myriad of people. The reuniting of people brought much joy, love, and happiness to both parties as they gave big, warm embraces and kisses.

Reflecting on these scenes made me think of the parallels in our relationship with God, our Father.

> Has there ever been a time when maybe you abandoned God thinking you didn't need Him in your life?

Have you been hurt by something difficult in your life or mad, blaming God for something that happened?

I bet God really wanted to give you a great big bear hug and let you know how much He loves you. And certainly that He misses you and hopes you return soon safely back to Him. I would even venture to say that God's heart is sad even though He really knows the whole picture.

REFLECTION:

Is something holding you back from being reunited with God?
How have you heard God calling you to Him?

> *"Jesus had compassion on them and touched their eyes. Immediately they received their sight and followed him."*
> ~ Matthew 20:34

49

Brokenhearted

One day as I was walking, a heart-shaped piece of blacktop caught my eye. Much to my dismay, the heart crumbled into three pieces as I picked it up. I was a little saddened and disappointed, but then I had two thoughts.

The first was, "break my heart for what breaks yours, God." I thought it was from a Bible verse, but it is a song lyric. It is a thought worth pondering.

What do you think breaks God's heart?

> Sinners who don't repent.
> The lost who have not heard the good news of Jesus.
> Those in society who are marginalized.
> Division in the Body of Christ.

It is a good reminder to look at our priorities to see how God is calling us to minister to those in need. Everyone is important to God and, because of God's love in us, we need to reach out to others. May our hearts be softened to see people as God does and to extend His compassion and love.

Lord, break my heart for what breaks yours. Inspire me to step out in faith, to minister to the least of my brethren. Amen.

The second thought was…

> *"The Lord is close to the brokenhearted; he rescues those whose spirits are crushed."*
> ~ Psalm 34:18 (NLT)

Finding this particular heart was apropos as I was praying for a friend whose mother was dying. I thought of the heartbreak they were experiencing in finding out only a few weeks earlier about her late-stage cancer.

This verse was also a reminder as I was trying to process the unexpected health news about a friend who was diagnosed with a brain tumor and was in treatment. My heart breaks for him and his family, especially his young children, as he learned about the growth of another tumor.

If the answer to our prayers is not what we want, it is difficult, especially in life and death situations. We need to hold tightly to our faith during these times.

Let's look at the passages surrounding the original verse.

> *"The Lord hears his people when they call to him for help. He rescues them from all their troubles. The Lord is close to the brokenhearted; he rescues those whose spirits are crushed. The righteous person faces many troubles, but the Lord comes to the rescue each time."*
> ~ Psalm 34:17-19 (NLT)

What encouragement do we receive from this Scripture?

> When God's children cry out to Him for help, He rescues them from their troubles.
> God is close to us when we are brokenhearted.
> He rescues our crushed spirits.
> The righteous face many troubles, but God comes to the rescue each time.

> *"The sacrifice you desire is a broken spirit. You will not reject a broken and repentant heart, O God."*
> ~ Psalm 51:17 (NLT)

We are encouraged knowing God does not reject us when our spirits are broken. He is with us during the tough times and when things don't go the way we want. What pleases God more than sacrifice is a humble heart who seeks Him even in the darkest trials. If we seek God wholeheartedly when we sin and repent, we receive His mercy.

The next day at church, my heavy heart was reminded to cling to God's word for comfort. We need to find His calm and peace, knowing God is in control as we lift each other trustingly to the Lord.

> *"God is our refuge and strength, an ever-present help in trouble."*
> ~ Psalm 46:1

> *"The Lord is my strength and shield. I trust him with all my heart. He helps me, and my heart is filled with joy. I burst out in songs of thanksgiving. The Lord gives his people strength. He is a safe fortress for his anointed king."*
> ~ Psalm 28:7-8 (NLT)

These verses remind us:

> God is our refuge.
> God is our strength.
> God is our shield.
>
> God is our ever-present help in trouble.
> We need to trust God with all our hearts.
> We have assurance God will help us.
>
> Our hearts are filled with joy, knowing God is helping us.
> We sing songs of thanksgiving to God.
> God is a safe fortress.

May these thoughts encourage you during the difficult trials of this life. Never stop praying and trusting the Lord. He is always with us and over everything.

REFLECTION:

What is one way your heart breaks for something God's heart does? Who is brokenhearted that God is leading you to minister to?

> *"Who redeems your life from the pit and crowns you with love and compassion."*
> ~ Psalm 103:4

50

Day By Day

Yes, day by day, even minute by minute, God does work everything out for our good.

I was transferred to a new position at my workplace because I wanted to retain my part-time status. When something not in "our" plan happens, we might not see God's hand at work in the situation until later. That was true in my case. However, I did feel God's hand providing this new position, especially as there are very few part-time positions available.

The blessing of less stress was a big plus. Interacting with different people was another one. Going from an environment of about five people to a room of at least 125 was a positive. It forced me to be friendlier, which has led me to make eye contact with people, smile, and say a friendly "good morning" or "hello." It has also translated into being friendly and encouraging to the four people I have daily email contact with who work from a satellite office.

A few months after starting the new position, I met one of the girls who worked from the satellite office, about an hour away. As that new friend is also a dance studio teacher, I had the pleasure of attending one of her recitals. Though I didn't get to talk with her that evening, it was fun doing something different.

Our daily work emails quickly progressed into getting to know one another personally with questions about one another's families. Being friendly has proven to make our working relationship better, in having one another's back as we verify our work.

One day, this new friend shared a song she was listening to, one that she choreographed a dance routine for. She asked if I knew the song "Day by Day" from the musical *Godspell*,[3] and suggested it would be a great song to pen some thoughts on. How could I refuse a challenge like that? I do believe the lyrics provide a great reminder about what we should keep our focus on as we go about living day by day.

"Day by Day" has a catchy tune with the lyrics repeating to help reinforce the thoughts. Though *Godspell* originally debuted off Broadway back in 1971, I believe the message of the song "Day by Day" has withstood the test of time. It is still applicable today.

The lyrics of the song that repeat are:

> *"Day by day*
> *Day by day*
> *Oh, Dear Lord*
> *Three things I pray*
> *To see thee more clearly*
> *Love thee more dearly*
> *Follow thee more nearly*
> *Day by day."*

What if we lived day by day, moment by moment, praying and living out the three main ideas mentioned in the song?

> TO SEE JESUS MORE CLEARLY…
> See clearly.
>
> > Do you see Jesus clearly day by day in…
> > nature?
> > others?
> > yourself?

>circumstances that occur in your life?
>the storms of your life?

To love Jesus more dearly...
>Love dearly.

>>Do you love Jesus dearly, day by day by...
>>continually offering praise to Him?
>>sharing the good news with others?
>>telling others of His goodness?
>>showing kindness in His name?
>>thanking Him for working in your life?

To follow Jesus more nearly...
>Follow nearly...

>>Do you follow Jesus more nearly day by day by...
>>reading Scripture?
>>praying unceasingly?
>>reading inspiring books or posts?
>>listening to encouraging music?
>>surrendering your life to Him?

Can I also challenge you to not only see, love, and follow Jesus day by day, but also to see, love and follow others who are a part of your life?

How about stretching yourself to see, love, and follow those who might not normally be a part of your circle of people?

Can you...

>See Jesus clearly...
>>in the poor person sitting on the street waiting for some coins to be thrown their way?

in the person who has no coat to keep warm?
in the person who is physically challenged needing a hand with their groceries?

Love dearly...
welcoming the stranger who looks different from you, maybe even having a noticeable physical ailment?
giving generously to help a person in a foreign country who needs a sponsor to help with the necessities of life?
the person who needs a ride to church?

Follow nearly...
to see someone you can pray with who needs help through a rough patch?
by sharing Christian music to help someone in their walk with the Lord?
through sharing an encouraging book or website that has helped you grow spiritually?

Be encouraged...

"Day by day
Day by day
Oh Dear Lord
Three things I pray
To see thee more clearly
Love thee more dearly
Follow thee more nearly
Day by day!"

REFLECTION:

Do you need to see, love, or follow Jesus more closely?
How can you share Jesus with someone today?

> *"He also came so that the Gentiles might give*
> *glory to God for his mercies to them.*
> *That is what the psalmist meant when he wrote:*
> *'For this, I will praise you among the Gentiles;*
> *I will sing praises to your name.'"*
> ~ Romans 15:9 (NLT)

51

Patches of Godlight

> *"Any patch of sunlight in a wood will show you something about the sun which you could never get from reading books on astronomy. These pure and spontaneous pleasures are 'patches of Godlight' in the woods of our experience."*
> ~ C.S. Lewis

A friend shared this quote. It has been a good exercise to think about what it means to me personally. We each may have a different interpretation based on our life experiences.

My thoughts turned to times I have seen the sun peeking through the darker, shaded woods. We experience the sunlight emerging in the darkness. We can read a book about the sunlight shining forth through the darkness, but it becomes real once we experience it ourselves. To read and visualize something is not the same as living it.

Three main points come to mind when I reflect on the quote:

LIFE IS ABOUT EXPERIENCES THAT SHAPE US.

In the woods of life, we learn the most when we experience God's presence and His love. We can read the Bible, but when we experience the meaning of the stories as they reach our hearts, we gain so much more.

> *"You make known to me the path of life; in your presence there is fullness of joy;*

> *at your right hand are pleasures forevermore."*
> ~ Psalm 16:11 (ESV)

Patches of Godlight are all around us.

Patches of Godlight might be an answer to what direction your life should be going. Maybe you are seeking a touch from God, knowing He is guiding your footsteps. Did God put a person in your path when you needed a prayer warrior? The good news is that God provides us with what we need when we need it. We need to be in tune to see how He provides.

> *"You, Lord, keep my lamp burning; my God turns my darkness into light."*
> ~ Psalm 18:28

Patches of sunlight bring us closer to the Son.

As we see and experience the patches of sunlight in our lives, we grow closer to Jesus. We encounter Jesus' presence with our eyes, the eyes of our hearts and soul. We get to know Him more intimately as we experience His power in our lives. We find joy in the simple ways we see His presence.

> *"Jesus spoke to the people once more and said, 'I am the light of the world. If you follow me, you won't have to walk in darkness, because you will have the light that leads to life.'"*
> ~ John 8:12 (NLT)

God provided an unexpected special patch of Godlight in my life recently. It was reconnecting with a friend I knew through volunteering as a candy striper when I was a teen. We hadn't seen each other in at least 25 years. It was a light-giving time of fellowship, sharing our love for the Lord with heart-to-heart discussions of Him. It was a pure and spontaneous pleasure in our woods of experience.

I encourage you to…

>be open to experiencing God's presence and love that reaches your heart.
>be aware of the patches of Godlight in your woods.
>come closer to Jesus as you experience the patches of sunlight in your life.

REFLECTION:

How has God provided patches of Godlight in your life this week? What have you learned about God through your experience?

> *"But because of his great love for us, God, who is rich in mercy, made us alive with Christ even when we were dead in transgressions— it is by grace you have been saved."*
> ~ Ephesians 2:4-5

52

Our Gifts

It is vital that we each share the gifts we have been given to help build up the Body of Christ of which we are a part. By doing that, we are working in harmony with our Creator to shine His love and mirror His image to the fellow pilgrims we journey with. It is easy to fall into the trap and lie of believing we don't have any special gifts to share. We do not have to go overseas to be a missionary to share our gifts.

We all have been given gifts to edify the Body of Christ and be used for God's glory.

> *"There are different kinds of gifts, but the same Spirit distributes them. There are different kinds of service, but the same Lord. There are different kinds of working, but in all of them and in everyone it is the same God at work. Now to each one the manifestation of the Spirit is given for the common good. To one there is given through the Spirit a message of wisdom, to another a message of knowledge by means of the same Spirit, to another faith by the same Spirit, to another gifts of healing by that one Spirit, to another miraculous powers, to another prophecy, to another distinguishing between spirits, to another speaking in different kinds of tongues, and to still another the interpretation of tongues. All these are the work of one and the same Spirit, and he distributes them to each one, just as he determines."*
> ~ 1 Corinthians 12:4-11

What do we learn from this Bible passage?
  The Spirit has given different kinds of spiritual gifts to us all.
  We all serve the Lord in our own unique way.

God works in all of us, and each of us has a special way of serving others.

Some spiritual gifts are...

>speaking with wisdom or knowledge.
>having great faith, the power to heal the sick, or to work mighty miracles.
>being a prophet, recognizing God's Spirit or a false spirit.
>speaking in different kinds of tongues and interpreting those tongues.

We don't decide which gifts are ours; the Spirit does.

"We have different gifts, according to the grace given to each of us. If your gift is prophesying, then prophesy in accordance with your faith; if it is serving, then serve; if it is teaching, then teach; if it is to encourage, then give encouragement; if it is giving, then give generously; if it is to lead, do it diligently; if it is to show mercy, do it cheerfully."
~ Romans 12:6-8

What do we learn from this Bible passage?
>God has given each of us different gifts to use.

Other gifts include...

>prophesy.
>serving others.
>encouraging others.
>giving to others.
>being a leader.
>being good to others.

When we use our gifts, they should always be used to the best of our ability and freely.

How can we identify our gifts if we are unsure of them?
> Asking trusted Christian friends what they see as our gifts.
> Discerning through prayer.
> Being open to opportunities God puts in your path.
> Special Spiritual Gift surveys.

It is important to remember a few things about our gifts…

> Sometimes, through the Holy Spirit, God calls us out of our comfort zone to utilize a gift. It might not be the gift we had in mind.
> He will always provide the avenue for us to use our gifts for His glory. Through the years, God may want us to use different gifts from our usual ones.
> God will always equip us with what we need to share our gifts.
> The gifts we are given are from God to further His kingdom and give Him glory.
> These gifts are not our power. It is God working through us and all credit goes to God.

I challenge you to dig deeper and see how daily you can use the gifts God has given you to make a difference. The gifts that God has given you are unique and make this world a better place.

I believe currently God has me utilizing the gifts of…

SHARING HIM AND MY HEART
> Through sharing weekly reflections. I was inspired to start writing simpler prose about God when I was in my late teens. I took a hiatus while raising my family. God has worked in my life to resurrect writing in recent years.

SERVING OTHERS

Serving others started when I was a teen and volunteered at a local hospital. From there, I came to help my great aunt with her finances and whatever she needed as her eyesight declined. Helping at a soup kitchen for many years now and helping in the dining area at retreats are other ways I am blessed to serve others.

ENCOURAGING OTHERS

When I see people who need extra prayer or are going through struggles, I try to offer them words of encouragement to brighten their day. Even at work, I try to keep in contact with co-workers at a different location that I have never met in person, just to encourage them and brighten their day.

REFLECTION:

What are the gifts God has given you?
How do you use them to edify the Body of Christ?

"God has given each of you a gift from his great variety of spiritual gifts. Use them well to serve one another."
~ 1 Peter 4:10 (NLT)

53

Perception

While walking outside daily, I continue to find hearts reminding me of God's love and care. They might be in the form of stones, blacktop, flowers, or whatever is around me. Hearts cross my path not only on my walks, but also at home, in stores, and even at the gas station.

I have noticed it depends on my perception or view whether the item looks like a heart. Sometimes when I pick up a stone, I position it in my hand based on different angles. One way, it might not look like a heart, but turning it a different way changes my perception of the shape. This makes me think of our relationship with God.

Our perception of life and its happenings are based on our experiences that form us into who we are and how we see the world.

> Our perception is key in how we see God and life.
> Our perception is key in how we handle the difficulties of life.
> Sometimes our perception is incorrect.
> Sometimes our perception is not reality.
> Sometimes our perception needs to be changed.

Isn't our faith a key factor that influences our perception of things in life?
> How do we handle the heartbreaks we endure?
> How do we make it through the losses we experience?
> How do we rise above the negativity we see?

"When he was alone, the Twelve and the others around him asked him about the parables. He told them, 'The secret of the kingdom of God has

been given to you. But to those on the outside everything is said in parables so that, they may be ever seeing but never perceiving, and ever hearing but never understanding; otherwise they might turn and be forgiven!'"
~ Mark 4:10-12

These verses come right after Jesus tells the parable of the sower found in Mark 4:1-9. This passage shows the importance of faith in our lives. Those who have faith in God and seek Him with sincere hearts are given the secret to the kingdom of God. Those with hearts hardened to faith are not able to perceive and understand the parables Jesus shared.

Our perception in life should be in alignment with God's view and His Word, which is truth.

What are instances when we might need to change our perception?

WHEN WE THINK WE AREN'T VALUABLE OR GOOD ENOUGH.

"Look at the birds of the air; they do not sow or reap or store away in barns, and yet your heavenly Father feeds them. Are you not much more valuable than they?"
~ Matthew 6:26

WHEN WE THINK GOD WON'T PROVIDE FOR US.

"And my God will supply every need of yours according to his riches in glory in Christ Jesus."
~ Philippians 4:19 (ESV)

WHEN WE THINK WE ARE ALONE.

"This is my command— be strong and courageous! Do not be afraid or discouraged. For the Lord your God is with you wherever you go."
~ Joshua 1:9 (NLT)

When the cares of this world weigh us down.

"Set your minds on things that are above, not on things that are on earth."
- Colossians 3:2 (ESV)

As you go about your day, take time to see if your perception of something needs an adjustment.

When my children were youngsters, my mother-in-law would take my daughter and turn her around three times to give her an "attitude adjustment." Maybe we need to do something similar when we find our perception needs some adjusting. Take time to adjust your perception if need be.

Remember to…

> stand firm in your faith.
> stand on the Word of God.
> strive daily for a Godly perception.
> don't be afraid to change your perception.

May your perception be more Godly each day as you stay rooted in the Word of God.

REFLECTION:

Did the Lord bring to mind something you need to adjust your perception on?
What truth spoke to your heart?

*"Do not remember against us our former iniquities;
let your compassion come speedily to meet us, for we are brought very low."*
- Psalm 79:8 (ESV)

54

Mission Reflections

Do you have a bucket list?
Are several items on it?

The one item on my bucket list is to participate in a short mission trip not too far away.

On a Christian music cruise, I was excited to learn about a one-day mission trip in the port of call. I assisted at the Bermudian Landing Baptist Church in Belize, where we made food bags for people in the village. It was a one-hour ride on a school bus throughout the streets of Belize, mostly remote, to arrive at our destination.

We were warmly welcomed with outstretched arms and hugs by the church greeters. The pastor invited us to participate in praise and worship, explaining the mission trip workers would be dismissed before the sermon began.

The pastor's daughter led the singing. I was brought to tears when she said, "Those in the front go to the back and greet your neighbor in love; those on the left go to the right." Seeing the whole church reach out to hug and greet one another was an amazing act of love that I treasure. Isn't that what we should be doing to all our brothers and sisters in the Lord?

Sitting two rows in front of me were three precious boys with beautiful dark eyes and wide smiles. When I hugged them, the youngest boy wouldn't let me go; yes, he warmed and stole my heart!

Then it was time to make the food bags. Learning that 90% of the people in the surrounding villages are unemployed and come to the church looking for food made our small time commitment more meaningful.

Through money donated to the foundation that sponsored the mission trip, the church was able to buy the food which was provided in the food bags. We measured out ten pounds of sugar, flour, and rice, and three pounds of beans, along with other food staples. There were several volunteers helping, so it did not take long.

I then went to the lunch preparation area. Some women had lovingly made chicken, rice, and beans, coleslaw, and cut-up watermelon for all the volunteers and church attendees. We helped carry the containers to the church and prepare the beverages.

At the end of the church service, I wanted to help distribute some of the bags to nearby villages and stretch myself to pray with the families. I saw a need to help someone fill the beverages from the cooler first, so hopped in to assist.

At one point, I went to see if the bus was ready to leave so we could distribute the food. I was disappointed to learn that another vehicle had already left to go to the houses. This resulted in me talking with the man who oversaw the mission trips. He genuinely apologized that I missed the opportunity to go. Our paths crossed a little later. He apologized again and asked if I was okay. He reminded me of the truth that life is so much about perspective.

> He said that maybe someone distributing the food bags needed the blessing more than me.
> He shared that his life was blessed through our conversation (as well as mine).

> His words reminded me of this recurring theme throughout the cruise in different situations.

"The mind of man plans his way, but the Lord directs his steps."
- Proverbs 16:9 (NASB)

Sometimes what we think we need or want is not what the Lord has planned. And that is okay.

As I shared with him that it seemed I did so little on the mission trip and that it was such a short amount of time, he also pointed out a few things.

> The church and village people will remember our PRESENCE more than anything. They will remember that we took time to be physically present with them; not the length of time or amount of work we did.
>
> Through our support of the mission trip, we helped provide food for people who otherwise would not have been blessed in this way.

Do you, too, need a reminder of some of the truths I learned?

> No act of kindness, done unto the Lord, is too small or unimportant.
> Every little thing we do has an impact on others.
> Surrender each situation to the Lord knowing He is working things out in His way.
> Your presence in others' lives is of paramount importance.
> Keep in mind we are not in control of life; God is.
> The importance of praying for the hearts and people you interact with.

I am grateful for the opportunity to have served on a short mission trip to that little church, and hope that someday I will be able to do a longer mission trip. How blessed we are when we extend ourselves in service and love to one another, especially to those who cannot repay us.

It is also important to realize that every day can be considered a mission trip.

I encourage you to view your daily life as such. God provides endless opportunities for us to serve, help, and bless others if we seek Him.

REFLECTION:

What mission field are you embarking on this day?
What gesture of love can you share with someone today?

> *"...For in you the fatherless find compassion."*
> ~ Hosea 14:3

55

Waiting

In life, we oftentimes spend a lot of time waiting for things.

Waiting...

> in line at the grocery store.
> to get gas for your car.
> for your car to be fixed.
> for a friend to get off the phone.
> for someone to stop and visit you.
> for a repairman to fix something.
> for the school day or the workday to end.
> for vacation to start.
> for the day you can get your license.
> for the day you will get married.
> for your first child to arrive.

We can learn some things in our waiting. Sometimes the Lord may be showing us...

> we need to slow down a little and shift our focus to Him.

We can do this, especially when we're waiting in lines.

> Have you ever said a short prayer for the cashier or taken a moment to talk to the person next to you in line? Try it next time you are waiting; you will be blessed, as well as blessing another.

I think it is also interesting to think about how the Lord could also be calling us to reflect on how He waits for us so patiently...

> for us to recognize Him in our lives.
> to surrender our lives to Him.
> to talk to Him.
> to spend time with Him.
> to recognize Him in our lives.
> to accept the great love He has for us.

REFLECTION:

What is something you learned while waiting for something from the Lord?

What situation did the Lord wait patiently for you?

> *"So the Lord must wait for you to come to him so he can show you his love and compassion. For the Lord is a faithful God. Blessed are those who wait for his help."*
> ~ Isaiah 30:18 (NLT)

56

Working Together in Harmony

Have you ever thought about how all the things in this world work together in harmony? As humans, but made in God's image, we need to look for ways to work in harmony and make this world a better place for others.

"Live in harmony with one another.
Do not be proud, but be willing to associate with people of low position.
Do not be conceited."
~ Romans 12:16

I think that is how God wants us to be with one another. We should help each other live in harmony, whether through an encouraging word, physically helping, praying, or sharing some gift we have.

This thought of things working together in harmony occurred to me when I was attending a Philharmonic concert. It amazes me to see how, with the vast amount of people and instruments in an orchestra or band, such great music is the result. I am in awe of how everyone knows exactly the right time to come in and play their own parts. So many instruments and different people from all walks of life can work perfectly together and play beautiful, harmonious music.

Think about how God made all of nature to work together in harmony. From the trees to the flowers, to the animals, to the birds of the sky, each has its own job and purpose on this earth. Snakes help reduce rodent populations, and mosquitoes are a great food source for birds, fish, and frogs, among other creatures. They all live together in harmony.

Think about the oceans and how the many creatures there live in harmony. Each creature in the sea exists to live in harmony and fulfill a purpose. There are even major ecosystems making beautiful coral reefs for our eyes to behold.

If you have a career, think about how smoothly things work when people work together in harmony. Being respectful and caring in our interactions, rather than demanding or mean, is one way to work more harmoniously. How about letting people think about and have a say in the way something could work better? Maybe the "lowly" person in the company holds the key to improving a process and saving the company money. Working together in harmony is much more beneficial.

In your home, especially if you have children, life is much better if you can find ways to live in harmony. If the kids are always fighting or arguing, life can be so draining, and it doesn't benefit anyone.

Our churches should be places where people feel welcome with a sense of community, where love is the center of everything that is done. People should pray for one another and help each other in whatever way they need. No one should be in need of physical things. Having programs to enrich and grow in our faith are important things to help us live more harmoniously.

Reaching out to a stranger through a smile, inviting a friend for dinner when they are alone, or sending a card can brighten someone's day. You just might be the one God uses to help another see something in a different light. It might change their life for the better, enabling them to live a life of harmony.

I am in awe of how God can use every event and circumstance in our lives to affect another. It might be to benefit you in some way, or maybe it was just what the other person needed. It is powerful to see how everything is connected. I can help you, you can help me, and together we can glorify the Lord in all we do and say.

Be open to seeing the Lord working in all of creation and to live in harmony with one another.

REFLECTION:

What is one way you helped someone live in harmony?
How did someone help bring harmony to your life?

> *"Finally, all of you, live in harmony with one another; be sympathetic, love as brothers, be compassionate and humble. Do not repay evil with evil or insult with insult, but with blessing, because to this you were called so that you may inherit a blessing."*
> ~ 1 Peter 3:8-9

57

The Radiance of God

A friend gave me a unique gift, which was a heart-shaped piece of wood that formed because of two trees growing together. On one side of the heart, there is a heart ingrained in the wood. My friend suggested preserving the heart.

My husband graciously sanded the heart a few times until it seemed perfected, making it smooth as silk, and getting rid of all the rough and dirty areas. He then spray-painted it with clear enamel. The wood kept soaking in the enamel, so several coats were needed to give it the beautiful luster it has now.

The heart displays even more beauty and vibrancy now. The grain of the wood and the cracks, made naturally while the wood was settling, are accented even more. The process of preserving this masterpiece of God's great love made me think of the parallels of our relationship with Him. God always loves us unconditionally, but He also wants us to grow deeper in our relationship with Him, as well as in our personal growth.

GOD REFINES US.

> *"These have come so that the proven genuineness of your faith— of greater worth than gold, which perishes even though refined by fire— may result in praise, glory and honor when Jesus Christ is revealed."*
> ~ 1 Peter 1:7

God refines our character, which helps to build our faith. It is not always pleasant, but we can give glory to God as we see Christ revealing Himself in our lives.

God smooths out our rough edges while drawing us closer to Him.

> *"The path of the righteous is level;*
> *you, the Upright One, make the way of the righteous smooth."*
> ~ Isaiah 26:7

We are brought to oneness with God and made righteous as God smooths our rough edges.

God makes us shine.

> *"Arise, shine, for your light has come, and the*
> *glory of the Lord rises upon you."*
> ~ Isaiah 60:1

God's glory shines through us as we continually draw closer to Him.

We need to be continually saturated with God's Word.

> *"Fix these words of mine in your hearts and minds;*
> *tie them as symbols on your hands and bind them on your foreheads."*
> ~ Deuteronomy 11:18

God's Word needs to be in our hearts and minds to help keep our focus.

Be reminded to let God…

> refine you.
> smooth your rough edges.

    make you shine.
    saturate you with His Word.

God puts the finishing touches on our lives to make us shine for His glory.

Let the radiance of God shine through you.
    Be beautiful and vibrant with God's glory.

REFLECTION:

How do you radiate God's Light?
What has God refined in your life?

> *"If it is to encourage, then give encouragement;*
> *if it is giving, then give generously;*
> *if it is to lead, do it diligently; if it is to show mercy, do it cheerfully."*
> *~ Romans 12:8*

58

Rainbow Reflections

It was a wonderful blessing to attend a retreat at one of my Holy Places on Canandaigua Lake. God is good and faithful, revealing His presence and love to us through His Word, the beauty of nature, and the people He puts in our path.

One afternoon and evening, I enjoyed spending time alone outside, viewing the beautiful scenery. The lake was tranquil, the sun was out for a bit, and some darker clouds moved in one part of the sky.

Much to my surprise, I heard thunder in the distance. I was gazing upon the area of sunlight, and when I turned the opposite way, I could see what looked like sheets of white reaching from the sky to the ground. I knew without a doubt a rainbow would soon appear. I grew anxious with expectation as I love to see God's presence in a rainbow. Sure enough, God did not disappoint as I soaked up the God moment.

Two rainbows emerged a little into the sky and then the one grew bigger where I could almost see the opposite end of it. I stood on the open grassy field as it started sprinkling. A few minutes later, a gentleman who assists at the retreat house and I sought shelter under the nearby gazebo, in awe of the rainbow. It provided a time of fellowship as we talked about some of his journey and marveled at God's masterpieces of creation. I felt inspired to give him one of my books, which was a bonus.

It became a little chilly and windy as the torrential downpour continued for maybe ten or fifteen minutes. The rain and fog were so intense that we could not see the lake in front of us until the sky got brighter and the rain lessened. Suddenly the dark sky was replaced by a crack of light, until at last, it illuminated the sky in brightness once more.

Two things stood out to me as the scene unfolded.

First, how interesting to think about how the sunlight reflects on the dark part of the sky where the rainbow then appears. The light of the sun reflecting upon the darkness creates a beautiful hue of colors, resulting in a rainbow.

> *"In the beginning the Word already existed. The Word was with God, and the Word was God. He existed in the beginning with God. God created everything through him, and nothing was created except through him. The Word gave life to everything that was created, and his life brought light to everyone. The light shines in the darkness, and the darkness can never extinguish it."*
> ~ John 1:1-5 (NLT)

The Word, Jesus, existing from the beginning, brings light into everything on this earth and to everyone. Light overcomes darkness, the Light that is Jesus. Jesus has overcome darkness. There is victory with Jesus.

> *"For you were once darkness, but now you are light in the Lord. Live as children of light (for the fruit of the light consists in all goodness, righteousness and truth.)"*
> ~ Ephesians 5:8-9

We were once in darkness before we came to accept and know Jesus. What a privilege we have living as children of the Light, of Jesus!

Second, how often in the storms of life we can't see anything until eventually the storm lightens up and light shines through. The light may just be a crack to begin with, but the light calms the raging storm.

> "Then he (Jesus) got into the boat and his disciples followed him. Suddenly a furious storm came up on the lake, so that the waves swept over the boat. But Jesus was sleeping. The disciples went and woke him, saying, 'Lord, save us! We're going to drown!' He replied, 'You of little faith, why are you so afraid?' Then he got up and rebuked the winds and the waves, and it was completely calm. The men were amazed and asked, 'What kind of man is this? Even the winds and the waves obey him!'"
> ~ Matthew 8:23-27

Jesus is the only One who has the power to control the winds and storms in our lives, just as He did on the lake with His disciples. Yes, Jesus can calm the storms in our lives when we reach out to Him. Sometimes Jesus doesn't take the storm away, but we can trust Him and be assured He is walking with us through the storm.

> "When you pass through the waters, I will be with you; and through the rivers, they shall not overwhelm you; when you walk through fire you shall not be burned, and the flame shall not consume you."
> ~ Isaiah 43:2 (ESV)

What encouragement we have knowing that no matter what storm we are walking through, it will not overtake us. Jesus is with us every step of the way.

May you be encouraged to…

> know the Light, Jesus, has overcome darkness.
> know the Light is triumphant.
> let the crack of Light calm your storm.
> know the Light, Jesus, is with you through the storms.

> "Try to be a rainbow in someone's cloud."
> ~ Maya Angelou

*"I kind of view everybody like a rainbow.
Everybody on the planet has all the colors of the rainbow inside."*
~ Alexia Fast

REFLECTION:

How does your life reflect the Light of Jesus?
How can you let the Light of Jesus break through the storms of life?

"No longer will you need the sun to shine by day, nor the moon to give its light by night, for the Lord your God will be your everlasting light, and your God will be your glory."
~ Isaiah 60:19 (NLT)

59

God Day

I want to share a simple yet profound thought I heard at a retreat. It will also serve as a challenge.

What does it mean when we say, "Good morning, good afternoon, good evening, good night, or even good day" to someone? I believe in all these cases we are expressing "good wishes" to the person for whatever time of day it is.

Don't we wish even more for the person?

What if we say instead…

> God morning…
> God afternoon…
> God evening…
> God night…
> God day…

Aren't our wishes for the people we encounter more about wishing God's…

- presence,
- love,
- mercy,
- joy,
- goodness,
- strength,
- blessings,

and compassion
to be with them throughout their day?

Are you up for the challenge of trying to greet people with the word "God" instead of "Good?"

It might be more difficult than you think to say, "God morning!" At least it was for me. I had to stop and consciously concentrate on saying "God" instead of "Good." During a break at the retreat, I tried it when I approached the speaker. If you send it in a text or email to someone, they might think you mistyped your message. However, if you continue to do it, they will get the idea it is intentional.

What are some Bible passages that mention morning, noon, and night?

> *"Lord, be gracious to us; we long for you.*
> *Be our strength every morning, our salvation in time of distress."*
> ~ Isaiah 33:2

> *"Morning, noon, and night I cry out in my*
> *distress, and the Lord hears my voice."*
> ~ Psalm 55:17 (NLT)

> *"At midnight I rise to give you thanks for your righteous laws."*
> ~ Psalm 119:62

> *"It is good to give thanks to the Lord, to sing praises to the Most High.*
> *It is good to proclaim your unfailing love in the morning,*
> *your faithfulness in the evening."*
> ~ Psalm 92:1-2 (NLT)

From these verses, what else will we include in our "God wishes?"

That people…

> know how gracious the Lord is.
> long for the Lord.
> turn to God in their distress.
> know the Lord hears their cry.
> give thanks to the Lord.
> sing praises to God.
> proclaim His unfailing love.
> know the Lord's faithfulness.

My sincere prayer for you is that you may have a "God day!"

Share "God wishes" as you go about your day.

REFLECTIONS:

Who is the first person you will say "God day" to?
Which God wish is most important to you?

> *"This is the day that the Lord has made;*
> *let us rejoice and be glad in it."*
> ~ Psalm 118:24 (ESV)

60

Silence

The first day of school for my youngest son started with him in the middle of a shower when the power went out. Our house has a well not city water, so when the power goes out, we do not have water. Thankfully, it was only for a few hours.

That morning, glancing at the clock, I thought, I have a few more minutes before I should make sure my son is up, so I laid back down. When I looked at the clock again, all I could see was darkness— no numbers were lit up. At first I thought my eyes were playing tricks on me, but then I realized the power was out. Suddenly, the stillness of silence was noticeable. Everything was just silent— no noise of anything electrical running, no music, not a peep.

The deafening silence occurred again a few hours later as a friend and I were at the local coffee shop. The silence was very noticeable there. Suddenly the lights went out, the TV was silent, and all the machines stopped working, no longer making their usual noises.

Can you recall a time when you lost power and suddenly everything was just silent? Isn't pure silence kind of eerie?

Aren't we so used to always being busy, hearing car engines, air conditioners, electronic devices, and the list goes on and on, that it is kind of scary to hear nothing?

As I observed and thought about how everything was suddenly so silent, I couldn't help but think that...

God was still there. He is present in the deafening silence.

In the deafening silence, can you sense the Lord?

Can you **hear** the stillness of the Lord's presence whispering to you?

> *"And your ears shall hear a word behind you, saying,*
> *"This is the way, walk in it," when you turn to*
> *the right or when you turn to the left."*
> ~ Isaiah 30:21 (ESV)

Can you **feel** the Lord's presence all around you?

> *"He is before all things, and in him all things hold together."*
> ~ Colossians 1:17

Can you **taste** the goodness of the Lord's presence?

> *"Taste and see that the Lord is good…"*
> ~ Psalm 34:8

Can you **see** the beauty of the Lord's presence?

> *"The heavens declare the glory of God; the skies*
> *proclaim the work of His hands.*
> ~ Psalm 19:1

Can you **smell** the fragrance of the Lord's presence?

> *"Live a life filled with love, following the example of Christ.*
> *He loved us and offered himself as a sacrifice*
> *for us, a pleasing aroma to God."*
> ~ Ephesians 5:2 (NLT)

Take a few more moments to cherish the silence and find the Lord's presence.

REFLECTION:

How do you experience God's presence in the silence?
Which of the five senses do you most often experience the Lord's presence?

"Where can I go from your Spirit? Where can I flee from your presence? If I go up to the heavens, you are there; if I make my bed in the depths, you are there. If I rise on the wings of the dawn, if I settle on the far side of the sea, even there your hand will guide me, your right hand will hold me fast."
~ Psalm 139:7-10

61

Gratitude

What do we do when overcome with grief? How about the times we experience despair?

As Christians, what are ways we can deal with grief and despair?
>Turn to Scripture for comfort.
>Pray.
>Share with a trusted friend who can encourage.
>Take a walk in nature.
>Share with the Lord.
>Cry when we need to.
>Seek Godly counsel.
>Express ourselves through music, artistry, or writing.
>Express gratitude to God.

Wait a minute! What was that last one mentioned? Yes, have you ever considered expressing gratitude to God when you are experiencing grief and despair?

Honestly, it was not something I ever considered until hearing my pastor, especially at funerals, say,
>*"Gratitude is the antidote to grief and despair."*

Let's first look at some definitions to help us dig deeper. Google searches yielded the following:
>Grief– deep sorrow, especially that caused by someone's death.
>Despair– the complete loss or absence of hope.

Gratitude– the quality of being thankful; readiness to show appreciation for and to return kindness.

If we try fighting sorrow and loss with appreciation…

> we will find some positives.
> we can slowly become thankful for the little things.
> we can dwell less on the negative.

Can we find gratitude…

> in waking up to a new day?
> for the air we breathe?
> for the beauty of creation?
> for the people who care about us, lifting us in prayer?
> for the memories we hold dear to our hearts?
> in the hope of being reunited with loved ones again?
> for whatever amount of time we had?
> in knowing, as hard as it can be, God works everything out for our good?

Despite practicing gratitude, we…

> will still be sad,
> will still miss people,
> may only find a small glimmer of hope,
> but grief and despair will not overcome us.

When we are walking through the times of grief and despair, this Psalm is a great one to read and ponder:

"The Lord is my shepherd; I shall not want. He makes me lie down in green pastures. He leads me beside still waters. He restores my soul. He leads me in paths of righteousness for his name's sake. Even though I

> *walk through the valley of the shadow of death, I will fear no evil, for you are with me; your rod and your staff, they comfort me. You prepare a table before me in the presence of my enemies; you anoint my head with oil; my cup overflows. Surely goodness and mercy shall follow me all the days of my life, and I shall dwell in the house of the Lord forever."*
> ~ Psalm 23:1-6 (ESV)

What do we take away from this Psalm?
> We can joyfully trust in the Lord.
> The Lord leads us as a shepherd.
> The Lord provides for us.
> The Lord is always with us.
> The Lord comforts us.
> The Lord blesses us as we lack for nothing.
> The Lord always dwells with us.

All these promises are ways we can extend our gratitude to the Lord. As a starting point when grieving and experiencing despair, try repeating one of the simple phrases from the Psalm to express gratitude to the Lord. Other suggestions are to start a gratitude journal or have an accountability partner.

By focusing on gratitude, we can hold on to the promise God is still in control of our lives. We may not understand or comprehend what God is allowing to happen, but He is still with us and loves us.

May you be encouraged to practice gratitude in whatever circumstance you find yourself. Try to take one small step toward living,

> *"Gratitude is the antidote to grief and despair."*

REFLECTION:

What Scripture gives you comfort when dealing with grief? Which take-away from Psalm 23 speaks most to you?

> *"But giving thanks is a sacrifice that truly honors me.
> If you keep to my path, I will reveal to you the salvation of God."*
> ~ Psalm 50:23 (NLT)

62

Adventure of A Lifetime

Attending a local women's worship conference sparked a memory. As I find often, God's perfect timing to hear about this conference two days before it was scheduled blessed me greatly. The people were friendly and welcoming, though I knew no one. At the start of the second day, a lady who also did not know anyone started talking to me. As we conversed and sat together at lunch, we learned we have a mutual friend who lives in her housing development. They are in an exercise class together, though they never conversed up to this point.

Returning to my memory, I flashback to August 2012, when my oldest son, then 19 years old, planned our family vacation. We opted to do a more local vacation. Our itinerary consisted of a butterfly conservatory, larger-scale zoo, a diamond mine, glider rides, and skydiving. Yes, you read that correctly, skydiving!

This son is not an adventuresome person. He prefers to be in control of his body and his surroundings at all times, so this adventure was a shock to us all. Because he wanted to skydive, I was determined to do it, despite being afraid of heights, along with my husband.

As we were driving to the skydiving place, I was growing more skeptical and scared about what we had signed up for. I had no choice but to follow through. Sometimes we need to do something even though we are afraid.

Skydiving is done in tandem with a professional. They tell you when it is time to "walk" off the plane into the air when the plane is around 10,000 – 13,500 feet in altitude. Then you pay attention to the hand signals showing you when to pull the cord, which way to turn, and when to maneuver your legs to come in for the landing. You free fall for about 60 seconds, going about 120 mph. You spend another four to five minutes parachuting down to the ground before landing on your rear with your legs out in a sitting position in front of you.

Reflecting on the skydiving experience, I see how it is like our relationship with God.

GOD IS ALWAYS WITH US, LIVING IN TANDEM WITH US.

> We may try to leave Him, but He is always pursuing us.

GOD IS ALWAYS DIRECTING AND GUIDING US, THAT STILL SMALL VOICE, WORKING EVERYTHING OUT FOR OUR GOOD.

> We may feel He is not guiding, but maybe our perspective needs adjusting to see clearly.

WE CAN ALWAYS SEE GOD'S PRESENCE AND HIS BEAUTY ALL AROUND US; JUST OBSERVE THE MAJESTIC MOUNTAINS, THE SEASONS, THE CREATURES OF THE LAND, AND ALL OF NATURE.

> Sometimes we may not like a particular weather pattern, but God is still in charge of it all.

WE SHOULD STEP OUT IN FAITH, NOT LETTING FEAR TAKE OVER.

> Sometimes we need to do things when we are afraid; it really is okay and will help us grow.

WE NEED TO TRUST AND HAVE FAITH THAT EVERYTHING WILL WORK OUT.

Sometimes things don't work out according to our plan, but that is okay. We know God is in charge.

Skydiving was never on my bucket list, but looking back, I can say I am glad I did it. There is a sense of confidence that can be gained from doing something out of our comfort zone. Stretching ourselves helps us grow and experience even more adventures in this life.

Yes, the SKY'S THE LIMIT, which was the name of our skydiving place.

REFLECTION:

What was something you did that was outside your comfort zone? What did God teach you through that experience?

"For I can do everything through Christ, who gives me strength."
~ Philippians 4:13 (NLT)

63

A Time to Rest

One of the hardest things for me to do is take time to rest in the loving arms of my Lord. Do you have that battle too?

Doesn't it seem like we are programmed to always be doing something, trying to balance all the necessary activities we do? Working, going to school, taking care of family, attending events and meetings, going to the gym, church activities, and the list goes on and on. All these things are important parts of our lives. They provide us with opportunities to serve the Lord in all we do; doing all things unto Him. How much more important it is to take time to rest with and in the Lord, in His loving arms.

How often do we allow time for resting in our busy schedules?

After a five-week hiatus from being needed to love on babies in the NICU, I was inspired by the thought of rest as I was holding two different little ones. Being in the NICU is a holy place for me. Seeing the littlest of babies, some connected to tubes and machines, so tiny fighting for their lives reminds me of the sanctity and sacredness of life; how precious life is in all its stages. One week I was holding and feeding a little one that was only 3 lbs. 7 oz. What a miracle of life.

My thoughts went to the newborns who require special caregiving, as well as the opposite end of the spectrum, the elderly who may also need special care. The caregivers are indeed special people who sometimes devote their lives to taking care of their spouses, parents, children, or friends.

One day as I was going into the entrance to the hospital, there was a mom unloading an older handicapped teen in a wheelchair from her van, bringing her inside, and going back to park her van. The scene tugged at my heart as they had get-well balloons they were bringing to the girl's dad. I silently said a prayer for them all, imagining what a difficult road they must be on.

I was able to hold a five-week-old boy who had the most adorable smile and expressions while he was resting in my arms. He was so animated; it made me smile just looking at him for the half-hour I held him.

It was my honor to hold a little girl for over three hours who had been in the NICU for almost five months. She was still receiving oxygen and it would be a while before she was able to go home to join her parents and her twin. I held her two different times, and the second time we conversed for a while before she nodded off to sleep. She had the biggest brown eyes, with long eyelashes, that just stared at me, hardly blinking. As she lay in my arms, she finally fell asleep, but now and then, she would get fussy and squirm. I sang softly and talked to her letting her know everything was okay.

As this sweet girl was resting securely in my arms, I couldn't help but think that…

God is always waiting for us…

> to fall securely into His arms,
> comforting us,
> loving us,
> telling us everything is okay,
> just like I was doing for this sweet little girl.

We, or at least I, need to make more of an effort to rest in His arms.

What are some ways you can rest in the Lord?

Take time to walk in nature.
Take time to go to a chapel.
Take time to go into a room in your house and shut the door.
Engage in prayer or conversation with the Lord.
Take time to listen to Him.

What does resting in the Lord look like?

Surrendering our racing mind.
Letting Him just "hold" us.
Soaking up His love.
Trusting Him.
Remembering who we are in Him.
Receiving the peace that He provides.

What are some benefits of resting in the Lord?

We will end up growing in our relationship with Him.
We will be rejuvenated.
We will have a fresh perspective on life.
We will be enlightened.

REFLECTION:

What is your favorite way to rest in the Lord?
What has God taught you in your resting?

> *"Then Jesus said, 'Come to me, all of you who
> are weary and carry heavy burdens,
> and I will give you rest. Take my yoke upon you.
> Let me teach you, because I am humble and gentle at heart,
> and you will find rest for your souls.
> For my yoke is easy to bear, and the burden I give you is light.'"*
> ~ Matthew 11:28-30 (NLT)

64

God Incidents

Sometimes it is easy to get caught up in worldly happenings and in our day-to-day chores. We are working, running the kids to places, rushing to meetings, and doing church activities and we forget how near the Lord is, and how He is working in our lives.

It is important even with all these activities, to keep God forefront and see Him working in our lives, even in the little things. Isn't it good to look at all the things in our lives as really God incidents?

Isn't it true that everything that happens is really under God's control? That is why I prefer to call these perfectly timed interactions God incidents, not coincidences.

Stop and think about all the God incidents that happen in just one single day...

> Think about that special friend the Lord gave you— the one you can talk to so easily about anything— the one who knows how you feel without even saying anything.

> Think about the person the Lord put in your path when you had a problem on your hands— the one who helped when you had a flat tire or car trouble.

> Think about the time you were in a hurry, needed a close parking spot to run into the store quickly, and saw someone ready to pull out at the exact time.

Think about the time you needed prayer and sent a text to a friend. They responded right away to tell you they were praying for you.

Think about the deadline at work or the household chores you thought would never get done timely or work out, but did.

Think about the beautiful sunrise or rainbow you saw, when you were feeling so helpless, or a creature in nature that brought you a breathtaking moment.

Think about the time you and your spouse both thought at the same time that you should pay it forward.

In all these, it is the Lord who is there working things out for our best and prompting us to act. How great it is to stop and reflect on the Lord working in our lives. Everything that happens is a God-incident, not merely a coincidence. It is also important to share these God-incidents with others to give glory to God, increase others' faith, and share the goodness of the Lord.

Trust in Him— He is faithful and true.

REFLECTION:

What is the last God-incident you were aware of?
Did you give glory to God for His goodness?

> *"The Lord is good to everyone. He showers compassion on all his creation."*
> ~ Psalm 145:9 (NLT)

65

Dance in the Rain

*"Life is not about waiting for the storms to pass.
It's about learning to dance in the rain."*
~ Vivian Greene

I saw this quote which struck me, the day before I was waiting for a weather storm to pass. It was another sunny, humid day as I began my walk. Bringing an umbrella was not on my radar. Partway into my walk, I noticed a few darker clouds rolling in, yet was intrigued by the sun shining forth.

I had a hunch to look behind me, and that is when I saw a rainbow for the third day in two weeks. As always, I was mesmerized by its beauty and wished I could see more of it.

It was then some big raindrops dotted the pavement. I was walking on a city block where there was no place for shelter from the torrential downpour I found myself in. I tried to find a big tree for shelter, hoping for protection, but it did not work. I had no choice but to embrace the rain and enjoy it cooling me off for a bit. I did consciously think about trying to enjoy the moment soaking in the rain. There was nothing else I could do.

I had a long sleeve sweater with me, which I eventually put on to absorb some of the wetness. When the rain lightened up, I continued walking. I was persistent and finished my usual path despite the drops of wet dripping off my cap and the squishing of my sneakers.

> *"Life is not about waiting for the storms to pass.*
> *It's about learning to dance in the rain."*
> ~ Vivian Greene

There are great lessons in this saying to apply to our faith journey. Three main points we can try to incorporate into our lives are…

EMBRACE THE STORM.

> *"Immediately Jesus made his disciples get into the boat and go on ahead of him to Bethsaida, while he dismissed the crowd. After leaving them, he went up on a mountainside to pray. Later that night, the boat was in the middle of the lake, and he was alone on land. He saw the disciples straining at the oars, because the wind was against them. Shortly before dawn he went out to them, walking on the lake. He was about to pass by them, but when they saw him walking on the lake, they thought he was a ghost. They cried out, because they all saw him and were terrified. Immediately he spoke to them and said, 'Take courage! It is I. Don't be afraid.' Then he climbed into the boat with them, and the wind died down. They were completely amazed, for they had not understood about the loaves; their hearts were hardened. When they had crossed over, they landed at Gennesaret and anchored there. As soon as they got out of the boat, people recognized Jesus. They ran throughout that whole region and carried the sick on mats to wherever they heard he was. And wherever he went— into villages, towns or countryside— they placed the sick in the marketplaces. They begged him to let them touch even the edge of his cloak, and all who touched it were healed."*
> ~ Mark 6:45-56

Notice that Jesus "made" His disciples get into the boat. We need to keep in mind that storms are a natural part of life. They can help us grow in our faith journey if we embrace them.

Embrace the storms, knowing…

> Jesus is always present in the boat of your storm.
> your storm might give you compassion and empathy to help others in their storms.
> your storm can encourage others to touch the edge of Jesus' cloak.

ENJOY THE PRESENT, EVEN THE STORMS.

> *"Forget the former things; do not dwell on the past. See, I am doing a new thing! Now it springs up; do you not perceive it? I am making a way in the wilderness and streams in the wasteland."*
> ~ Isaiah 43:18-19

> *"Therefore do not be anxious about tomorrow, for tomorrow will be anxious for itself. Sufficient for the day is its own trouble."*
> ~ Matthew 6:34 (ESV)

God wants us to enjoy the present. We can't live waiting to enjoy life when there are no storms. We would never appreciate the beauty of the current moment.

Enjoy the present, knowing…

> Jesus is present in each moment.
> looking to the past prevents us from seeing the beauty God is providing today.
> dwelling on the future of things that might not happen is futile.

EXHIBIT AN ATTITUDE OF THANKSGIVING IN THE STORMS.

> *"Never stop praying. Be thankful in all circumstances, for this is God's will for you who belong to Christ Jesus."*
> ~ 1 Thessalonians 5:17-18 (NLT)

> *"And give thanks for everything to God the Father*
> *in the name of our Lord Jesus Christ."*
> ~ Ephesians 5:20 (NLT)

We need to cultivate a spirit of thanksgiving to be able to dance in the storms of life. We need to practice gratitude in all circumstances. God is so good and faithful if we look for Him.

Exhibit an attitude of thanksgiving knowing…

> Jesus is in charge of each moment.
> prayer brings us closer to God's presence.
> we can be grateful for the smallest of blessings.

I encourage you to focus on learning to dance in the rain. I pray you may find joy and peace in the storms of life as you dance.

Remember…

> Embrace the storms – Jesus is always present in the boat of your storm.
> Enjoy the present, even the storms – Jesus is present in each moment.
> Exhibit an attitude of thanksgiving in the storms – Jesus is in charge of each moment.

REFLECTION:

In what storm did you see God working powerfully in your life?
Did you embrace the storm with confidence or fight it?

> *"As you know, we count as blessed those who have persevered.*
> *You have heard of Job's perseverance and have seen*
> *what the Lord finally brought about.*
> *The Lord is full of compassion and mercy."*
> ~ James 5:11

66

A Day of Blessings

*God is present and can be found in every moment,
in every detail,
of our lives if we take the time to notice!*

I saw a write-up from a coworker about a basket raffle she was holding to help raise money to cover expenses for her brother. He, too, is an employee and recently suffered a stroke, and has an autoimmune disease. I felt I wanted to contribute a monetary donation to help, so I introduced myself. I did not know their thoughts about God. When I was getting the donation ready, I thought about bringing two of my "Treasured Verse" booklets in case I got a sense they could provide a little encouragement.

In our short conversation, she did mention God. I learned they were both believers, so I felt good giving her the booklets, which she would read to her brother. She said, "If my brother ever leaves the hospital, it will be a miracle." I started praying. She also mentioned that you can't give up hope.

I am happy to report that a miracle did happen. On Thanksgiving Day, he was cleared to go home, though given a six-month life expectancy. "Prayers are the first steps in miracles" is a quote I saw. I treasure that interaction and the privilege of being able to pray for her brother and the family, as well as getting updates on his progress.

As I walked in the door of an auto garage, I heard the gentleman at the desk ask a mechanic if he could drive a lady home. Only with God's perfect timing, which is always impeccable, did it happen to be a good friend. In fact, she calls my husband and me her "other children." Her husband is unable to drive, so dropping off a car presents an issue for her.

Without hesitation, I said, "I'll take her home" and then returned later to leave my car. My day had the bonus of spending a few minutes visiting with the couple. This gentleman lives in chronic pain every waking moment. Both of their attitudes are always positive, and they always care about others, making them feel special and loved.

When I returned to the garage to drop off my car, I had a lengthy, engaging conversation with the gentleman at the counter about God and faith in our lives. It is great to be able to share and learn from the experiences and views of others.

I struggle with making decisions and overthinking the possible outcomes. As I was walking home from the garage, I couldn't decide whether to take a little diversion to the coffee shop. Ultimately, my feet took me there. In doing so, the blessing I encountered was seeing a lady working there who had quit about six months earlier. My day is always brighter when I see her and the smile that is always on her face. I was surprised to see her and was happy to talk with her again.

May you experience God in the ordinary, mundane tasks of your life.

>Blessings can be found
>everywhere and in everyone
>because God is truly
>everywhere and in everyone!
>
>Yes, He truly is at work in every
>circumstance in our lives.
>Take time to see Him and
>praise Him for His goodness.

REFLECTION:

What unexpected encounter filled you with joy?
In what ordinary task did God reveal Himself?

> *"What if he did this to make the riches of his glory known
> to the objects of his mercy, whom he prepared in advance for glory—
> even us, whom he also called, not only from the
> Jews but also from the Gentiles?"*
> ~ Romans 9:23-24

Christine M. Fisher

67

Instruments of Love

How have experienced God's love?

Have you felt God's love through…

> the beauty of nature?
> viewing the ocean waters?
> worship music?
> inspiring writings?
> the quiet?
> those who serve you when you are in need?
> feeling valued and respected by another?
> the person who takes time to listen to not only your words, but also your heart?

I heard this quote from a sermon:

> *"If people sense that we **value** them, that we are **listening** to them, then we become the instruments by which they sense the **love of God**."*

How powerful is that statement?
>   Does it ring true in your life?
>>   Didn't Jesus model that quote?

By the way He valued and listened to people, Jesus was an instrument of the love of God to others.

> *"A man with leprosy came and knelt in front of Jesus, begging to be healed.*
> *'If you are willing, you can heal me and make me clean,' he said.*
> *Moved with compassion, Jesus reached out and touched him.*
> *'I am willing,' he said. 'Be healed!'*
> *Instantly the leprosy disappeared, and the man was healed."*
> ~ Mark 1:40-42 (NLT)

Jesus listened to the leper's earnest plea to be healed. Jesus valued this leper. He willingly touched him, which was something that would make Jesus unclean according to the Mosaic law. The leper was healed immediately and experienced God's love for him.

We know sometimes God has reasons for "not willing" to heal our bodies in the way we want. We should keep in mind that we are still valued and loved by Him. God is God, and we need to trust that His perfect will is at work in our lives.

> *"'Teacher,' they said to Jesus, 'this woman was caught in the act of adultery. The law of Moses says to stone her. What do you say?' They were trying to trap him into saying something they could use against him, but Jesus stooped down and wrote in the dust with his finger. They kept demanding an answer, so he stood up again and said, 'All right, but let the one who has never sinned throw the first stone!' Then he stooped down again and wrote in the dust. When the accusers heard this, they slipped away one by one, beginning with the oldest, until only Jesus was left in the middle of the crowd with the woman. Then Jesus stood up again and said to the woman, 'Where are your accusers? Didn't even one of them condemn you?' 'No, Lord,' she said. And Jesus said, 'Neither do I. Go and sin no more.'"*
> ~ John 8:4-11 (NLT)

This woman committed adultery, an offense that warranted stoning her according to the law of Moses. Jesus valued her as a child of God. He asked the teachers of the law and the Pharisees that whoever of them was without sin to cast the first stone. Jesus shared God's love with this woman by not condemning her but encouraging her to change her life and ways.

This acrostic describes some of Jesus' listening skills:

> **L**ove
> **I**ntently
> **S**incerity
> **T**enderly
> **E**mpathy
> **N**onjudgmental

How well do you measure up to Jesus' example?

> Is there one area above that you need to improve upon when listening to others?
> How can we model Jesus' listening to others?

How can we better share God's love by listening and making others feel valued?

By…

> giving our full attention to the person.
> letting our hearts hear what the person is sharing.
> ridding our mind and heart of prejudices.
> asking engaging, open-ended questions.
> not interrupting.
> showing patience.
> trying to empathize.
> validating what the person is feeling.
> praying with the person.

May you be encouraged to...

> work on one word from the acrostic to better model how Jesus listened.
> be instruments of love,
> > of God's love,
> > > as you strive to listen from the heart,
> > > > helping others feel valued.

*"If people sense that we **value** them, that we are **listening** to them, then we become the instruments by which they sense the **love of God**."*

REFLECTION:

Who do you sense the love of God through by the way they value and listen to you?
Which word from the acrostic do you need to work on most?

*"My dear brothers and sisters, take note of this:
Everyone should be quick to listen, slow to speak and slow to become angry."*
~ James 1:19

Section 4

GOD'S COMPASSION ILLUMINATED IN THE HOLY LAND

"'And they will be mine,' says the Lord of armies, 'on the day that I prepare my own possession, and I will have compassion for them just as a man has compassion for his own son who serves him.'"
~ Malachi 3:17 (NASB)

God's goodness in my life graced me with an opportunity to walk in Jesus' footsteps in the Holy Land in February 2022. It was a treasured adventure to experience the different sites that are significant and central to our faith.

The timelessness of God's Word was impressed upon my heart while walking where Jesus did over 2000 years earlier. Despite our current world with all its technical advances, God's Word still applies to us.

I cannot help but think that God sending Jesus to walk this earth, in both divine and human form, is one of the greatest acts of God's compassion. We have a Savior who understands our humanity and can relate to us.

In this section, I pray you will experience your own Holy Land pilgrimage as I walk you through the lessons, experiences, and insights I gained while walking where Jesus did.

At the end of each reflection, I have included a web address where you can see more pictures, in full color, of the different sites. Many of the reflections from the book are combined into one on the website.

God's compassion illuminated in the Holy Land.

"When the sunshine of loving kindness meets the raindrops of suffering, the rainbow of compassion arises."
~ Clive Holmes

68

The Fifth Gospel

I am so grateful to have experienced a trip of a lifetime to the Holy Land. I never imagined having the opportunity to experience Israel, but it was a wonderful ripple effect of God's orchestrations.

I am in awe that I walked in some of the very same places Jesus did more than 2000 years ago. Our tour guide and hosts shared vast knowledge and insights about the places we saw and Jesus' life. It has given me a lot to reflect on.

I want you to be able to join in and experience what St. Jerome said:

> *"Five gospels record the life of Jesus.*
> *Four you will find in books and the one you*
> *will find in the land they call Holy.*
> *Read the fifth gospel and the world of the four will open to you."*
> ~ St. Jerome (347-420 A.D.)

It is appropriate to start with background information. This trip was supposed to happen in January 2021 but, due to the pandemic, was postponed until January 2022. Things were not looking favorable for travel to Israel about a week and a half before our departure date. A week before the trip, God worked things out so that a smaller group of those wishing to travel could go. Our group was the first group to enter Israel after the two-year shutdown due to the pandemic. There were only a few times we encountered another group at the same place.

One blessing was the fact we did not have to wait in line to see the sites. Usually, the wait is an hour or two to get in. It was nice to be able to visit a place more than once since there was no waiting. We were the only group at each of the two guesthouses where we stayed, so we were free to wander around. We stayed in both Galilee and Jerusalem. Galilee is in northern Israel and Jerusalem is in the southern part.

I felt strongly that I was supposed to go on this trip at this point in my life. God proved this to me through His undeniable peace and with the way He seemed to work everything out perfectly in my life. My hope is that I will fulfill all that God has planned for me through this experience.

As we embarked on the pilgrimage, I wrote,

> "My hope for this trip is to be in awe of walking where Jesus did, seeing the places He lived and walked. I also hope I return a different person. May I meet Jesus in an even deeper way through walking in His footsteps, with Him being even more real to me. I am so blessed and grateful for this opportunity."

> My prayer was that the pilgrimage would change the core of my being, making me more like Christ.

I have never been one to know much about historical things, so I learned a lot on this pilgrimage about

THE HISTORY OF ISRAEL AND THE LAND WE WALKED.

> Israel is only 2% Christian.
> The northern area is greener.
> The southern area is more desert.
> Of the Arabs in Palestine, 98% are Muslim and 2% are Christian.

THE SEA OF GALILEE.

>Is also known as the Lake of Gennesaret and Lake Tiberis.
>Is heart shaped.
>Is the largest freshwater source for Israel, providing its drinking water.

THE JORDAN RIVER.

>Is very muddy.
>Runs from the Sea of Galilee in the north to the Dead Sea in the south.
>Is the lowest point of any river in the world.

THE DEAD SEA.

>Is the lowest point of any place on earth.

JERICHO IS THE OLDEST CONTINUOUSLY INHABITED CITY IN THE WORLD.

A few of the highlights of the pilgrimage for me were…

>observing the vastness and beauty of the Judean Desert. It was truly breathtaking and awe inspiring to think of Jesus and John the Baptist there.

>seeing the Garden of Gethsemane and the rock where Jesus prayed if the cup of suffering could be taken from Him. A special memory was having a heart-to-heart conversation with a friend about faith that ended in prayer as we walked around this holy place.

>standing at the places where Mary was visited by the angel who announced she would be the mother of Jesus, Calvary where

Jesus hung on the cross to set you and me free, and the places where Jesus was buried and resurrected.

stretching myself to proclaim Scripture in Capernaum, where Jesus had proclaimed Scripture, and at the Holy Sepulchre, where Jesus died, was buried, and resurrected.

I believe this Scripture story entitled "Jesus' First Disciples" is fitting to apply to the pilgrimage.

> *"The next day John was there again with two of his disciples. When he saw Jesus passing by, he said, 'Look, the Lamb of God!' When the two disciples heard him say this, they followed Jesus. Turning around, Jesus saw them following and asked, 'What do you want?' They said, 'Rabbi' (which means "Teacher"), 'where are you staying?' 'Come,' he replied, 'and you will see.' So they went and saw where he was staying, and they spent that day with him. It was about four in the afternoon. Andrew, Simon Peter's brother, was one of the two who heard what John had said and who had followed Jesus. The first thing Andrew did was to find his brother Simon and tell him, 'We have found the Messiah' (that is, the Christ). And he brought him to Jesus. Jesus looked at him and said, 'You are Simon son of John. You will be called Cephas' (which, when translated, is Peter)."*
> ~ John 1:35-42

I see the pilgrimage to the Holy Land as Jesus' invitation to be one of His disciples and follow Him. Indeed, I know Jesus is the Lamb of God. I wanted to see where He stayed too. His invitation to *"Come, and you will see"* was to walk where He did, see the places He grew up in Nazareth, stand in the place He preached in Capernaum, see where He prayed in the Garden of Gethsemane, and so much more. Yes, I have found the Messiah, and I want to bring you along to meet Jesus more intimately through sharing my experience.

REFLECTION:

When have you experienced Jesus telling you to *"Come, and you will see?"* Who have you shared Jesus with?

> *"Go, walk through the length and breadth of the land, for I am giving it to you."*
> ~ Genesis 13:17

https://www.hopetoinspireyou.com/2022/03/01/a-holy-land-pilgrimage/

69

Mount Arbel

MOUNT HERMON

Today, we embark on our Holy Land pilgrimage. Are you relieved that you don't have to take the 9 and ½-hour plane ride? As we journey along, I hope the places and Scriptures come alive so you personally experience the fifth gospel. I encourage you to pause for a few minutes to think about and answer the reflection questions you will find along the way.

Mount Arbel, the first stop on our pilgrimage, is located in the Lower Galilee region and towers above the Sea of Galilee. I was fascinated to see the caves that were dug into the mountain, which were hideout places for the Jews who fought against the Greeks and Romans.

At the top of Mount Arbel, there is a great panoramic view of the surrounding land. You can see Mount Hermon, which was a snow-covered mountain range in the distance. Its summit is located on the Lebanon-Syria border. Some Scripture scholars believe the Transfiguration may have occurred at Mount Hermon.

> *"Six days later Jesus took Peter and the two brothers, James and John, and led them up a high mountain to be alone. As the men watched, Jesus' appearance was transformed so that his face shone like the sun, and his clothes became as white as light."*
> ~ Matthew 17:1-2 (NLT)

REFLECTION:

When have you witnessed Jesus being transfigured in your life?
When has His presence been so real to you that you experienced His brightness illuminating your faith journey?

CITY ON A HILL

While on Mount Arbel, viewing a city on a hill, we read and reflected on the following Scripture:

> *"You are the light of the world— like a city on a hilltop that cannot be hidden. No one lights a lamp and then puts it under a basket. Instead, a lamp is placed on a stand, where it gives light to everyone in the house. In the same way, let your good deeds shine out for all to see, so that everyone will praise your heavenly Father."*
> ~ Matthew 5:14-16 (NLT)

REFLECTION:

How are you a light in this world for God?
Whose path do you light up so they can praise God?

Landmark

A landmark at the top of Mount Arbel is a single tree, seen here. While riding around the area, it is a good identifier of Mount Arbel. How did God do that?

REFLECTION:

How do you bloom in the desert of life?
Do you stand out for God?

Mount arbel

Mount Arbel is not specifically mentioned in the Bible by name, but it is possible it is the mountain referenced in this passage:

> "Then the eleven disciples went to Galilee, to the mountain where Jesus had told them to go. When they saw him, they worshiped him; but some doubted. Then Jesus came to them and said, 'All authority in heaven and on earth has been given to me. Therefore go and make disciples of all nations, baptizing them in the name of the Father and of the Son and of the Holy Spirit, and teaching them to obey everything I have commanded you. And surely I am with you always, to the very end of the age.'"
> ~ Matthew 28:16-20

REFLECTION:

Hear Jesus say to you personally, *"Go and make disciples of all nations. And surely I am with you always."*
In what ways is Jesus calling you to share and make disciples for Him?

As I was the last person walking away from the view on the Mount, a few tears came to my eyes thinking of Jesus walking this land. I felt such gratitude to be experiencing this pilgrimage. I prayed the Lord would make me like that city on the hill and let my light shine for Him always. Use me, Lord. I heard the Lord remind me to *"go make disciples of all nations"* by continuing to share my heart through the written word. His reassurance that *"surely I am with you always, to the very end of the age"* brings me comfort. He is always walking with us!

As you reflect on our time at Mount Arbel, be encouraged to…

>let Jesus transform your life.
>let His light shine through you.
>bloom where you are planted.
>go make disciples for Him.
>know that Jesus is with you every step of the way.

>*"Praise be to the God and Father of our Lord Jesus Christ, the Father of compassion and the God of all comfort."*
>~ 2 Corinthians 1:3

https://www.hopetoinspireyou.com/2022/03/08/mount-arbel/

70

Nazareth

Look at a map of the Holy Land where you can locate some of the places we will visit on our pilgrimage: Nazareth, Bethlehem, Capernaum, Cana, Magdala, Tabgha, Bethsaida, the Sea of Galilee, the Jordan River, the Dead Sea, the Mediterranean Sea, Jerusalem, Mount of Temptation, Jericho, Masada, and Tel-Aviv.

While walking in the footsteps of Jesus, it is appropriate to start with a visit to the site where it all started. We begin our pilgrimage today in Nazareth, at the house where Mary, who would become the mother of Jesus, lived.

I felt the sacredness of being in this place as I gazed upon the actual site where Mary lived, caught in the moment of visualizing the angel Gabriel coming to a young teen girl. She had no idea how things would work, yet Mary gave us the perfect example of being open to God's will for her life. I enjoyed some extra free time here, reflecting on the Annunciation and Mary's "Yes" to God.

> *"In the sixth month of Elizabeth's pregnancy, God sent the angel Gabriel to Nazareth, a town in Galilee, to a virgin pledged to be married to a man named Joseph, a descendant of David. The virgin's name was Mary. The angel went to her and said, 'Greetings, you who are highly favored! The Lord is with you.' Mary was greatly troubled at his words and wondered what kind of greeting this might be. But the angel said to her, 'Do not be afraid, Mary; you have found favor with God. You will conceive and give birth to a son, and you are to call him Jesus. He will be great and will be called the Son of the Most High. The Lord God will give him the throne*

of his father David, and he will reign over Jacob's descendants forever; his kingdom will never end.' 'How will this be,' Mary asked the angel, 'since I am a virgin?' The angel answered, 'The Holy Spirit will come on you, and the power of the Most High will overshadow you. So the holy one to be born will be called the Son of God. Even Elizabeth your relative is going to have a child in her old age, and she who was said to be unable to conceive is in her sixth month. For no word from God will ever fail.' 'I am the Lord's servant,' Mary answered. 'May your word to me be fulfilled.' Then the angel left her."
~ Luke 1:26-38

REFLECTION:

Do you see yourself as the Lord's highly favored servant?
Do you trust God, letting Him work in your life without trying to figure everything out?

As you reflect on our pilgrimage stop in Nazareth, be encouraged to remember...

that you are the Lord's servant.

> *"The Lord, the God of their fathers, sent persistently to them by his messengers, because he had compassion on his people and on his dwelling place."*
> ~ 2 Chronicles 36:15 (ESV)

https://www.hopetoinspireyou.com/2022/03/15/jesus-humble-beginnings/

71

Bethlehem

We fast-forward nine months as we travel to Bethlehem, the place where Jesus was born. It is believed the 14-point star on the floor is the spot where Jesus was born. The star has a Latin inscription that says, "Here Jesus Christ was born to the Virgin Mary." The 14-point star represents the three sets of 14 generations in the genealogy of Jesus Christ. Because the Son of God became the Son of Man here, we are God's sons and daughters. Emmanuel, God is with us.

"Here Jesus Christ was born to the Virgin Mary."

A few feet away is the place where Jesus was laid in the manger, a feeding trough for animals.

> *"In those days Caesar Augustus issued a decree that a census should be taken of the entire Roman world. (This was the first census that took place while Quirinius was governor of Syria. And everyone went to their own town to register. So Joseph also went up from the town of Nazareth in*

Galilee to Judea, to Bethlehem the town of David, because he belonged to the house and line of David. He went there to register with Mary, who was pledged to be married to him and was expecting a child. While they were there, the time came for the baby to be born, and she gave birth to her firstborn, a son. She wrapped him in cloths and placed him in a manger, because there was no guest room available for them."
~ Luke 2:1-7

REFLECTION:

Does the inn of your heart need more room for Jesus?
Does your life reflect the same humility as Jesus' humble beginnings?

As you reflect on our pilgrimage stop in Bethlehem, be encouraged to remember…

Emmanuel, God is with you always.

*"He has caused his wonders to be remembered;
the Lord is gracious and compassionate."*
~ Psalm 111:4

https://www.hopetoinspireyou.com/2022/03/15/jesus-humble-beginnings/

72

Shepherd's Field

We journey now to a small town east of Bethlehem, to a place called Shepherd's Field. We enter a cave where the shepherds would have been busy tending to their flock when they received good news from an angel of the Lord. Shepherds were considered the lowly and poor ones in society, yet God chose them to be the first ones to learn about the birth of Jesus.

It was a powerful experience to be in the cave and put myself in the shepherd's place while hearing the angel's good news. Isn't it comforting to think how they were warned not to be afraid of seeing an angel, as angels were usually associated with death? Then they suddenly heard the heavenly host praising God. The shepherds were excited to go to Bethlehem to see the Messiah, which in turn made them glorify and praise God. They were the first evangelists.

> *"And there were shepherds living out in the fields nearby,*
> *keeping watch over their flocks at night. An*
> *angel of the Lord appeared to them,*
> *and the glory of the Lord shone around them, and they were terrified.*
> *But the angel said to them,*
> *'Do not be afraid. I bring you good news that*
> *will cause great joy for all the people.*
> *Today in the town of David a Savior has been born to you;*
> *he is the Messiah, the Lord. This will be a sign to you:*
> *You will find a baby wrapped in cloths and lying in a manger.'*
> *Suddenly a great company of the heavenly host appeared with the angel,*
> *praising God and saying, 'Glory to God in the highest heaven,*

> *and on earth peace to those on whom his favor rests.'*
> *When the angels had left them and gone into heaven,*
> *the shepherds said to one another, 'Let's go to Bethlehem and see*
> *this thing that has happened, which the Lord has told us about.'*
> *So they hurried off and found Mary and Joseph, and the baby,*
> *who was lying in the manger. When they had seen him,*
> *they spread the word concerning what had been told them about this child,*
> *and all who heard it were amazed at what the shepherds said to them.*
> *But Mary treasured up all these things and pondered them in her heart.*
> *The shepherds returned, glorifying and praising*
> *God for all the things they had heard and seen,*
> *which were just as they had been told."*
> ~ Luke 2:8-20

REFLECTION:

Do you react to the good news of Jesus with joy in your heart? Do you glorify and praise God for the way you see Him working in your life?

As you reflect on our pilgrimage stop at Shepherds Field, be encouraged to remember…

to give glory and praise to God for all He does in your life.

> *"Therefore, since through God's mercy we have*
> *this ministry, we do not lose heart."*
> ~ 2 Corinthians 4:1

https://www.hopetoinspireyou.com/2022/03/15/jesus-humble-beginnings/

73

Jordan River

Hello, my fellow pilgrims. We have arrived at the Jordan River, where Jesus' public ministry began when he was 30 years old. Jesus was baptized by His cousin, John the Baptist, whose mission was to call people to repentance in preparation for Jesus' coming. John baptized people in the Jordan River as they confessed their sins and repented.

Why did Jesus, the only one who never sinned, need to be baptized by John? There are four reasons we can glean from Scripture…

Jesus stated, "…*to fulfill all righteousness*." Righteousness is defined as "the quality of being made morally right or justifiable." Jesus was baptized to show He was consecrated to and by God.

It was a public announcement by John that Jesus was the Messiah.

Jesus identified Himself with man's sin and that He was our substitute.

An example for His followers.

The muddy Jordan River

"In those days John the Baptist came, preaching in the wilderness of Judea and saying, 'Repent, for the kingdom of heaven has come near.' This is he who was spoken of through the prophet Isaiah: 'A voice of one calling in the wilderness, "Prepare the way for the Lord, make straight paths for him."' John's clothes were made of camel's hair, and he had a leather belt around his waist. His food was locusts and wild honey. People went out to him from Jerusalem and all Judea and the whole region of the Jordan. Confessing their sins, they were baptized by him in the Jordan River."
~ Matthew 3:1-6

"Then Jesus came from Galilee to the Jordan to be baptized by John. But John tried to deter him, saying, 'I need to be baptized by you, and do you come to me?' Jesus replied, 'Let it be so now; it is proper for us to do this to fulfill all righteousness.' Then John consented. As soon as Jesus was baptized, he went up out of the water. At that moment heaven was opened, and he saw the Spirit of God descending like a dove and alighting on him. And a voice from heaven said, 'This is my Son, whom I love; with him I am well pleased.'"
~ Matthew 3:13-17

Reread that last sentence and reflect on its significance.

> *"And a voice from heaven said, 'This is my Son, whom I love; with him I am well pleased.'"*

Isn't it encouraging to see how God affirms His love for Jesus even before He began His public ministry or performed any miracles? How many times do we think we need to **do** something to earn God's love? This proclamation teaches us that we serve God **out** of His unmerited love for us. We cannot earn God's love. It is a free gift for us all.

REFLECTION:

Do you live daily knowing you, too, are consecrated to and by God? Have you thanked Jesus for His willingness to be your righteousness or sin substitute through His baptism and death on the cross?

> As a side note, you might not want to attempt to touch the Jordan River. I warn you from personal experience that it is very slippery and muddy. I stepped down on one of the two stairs to find the mud was too thick. One muddy sneaker made me decide not to touch the river. Three weeks later, I finally got the mud removed.

As you reflect on our pilgrimage to the Jordan River, be encouraged to remember…

> you are consecrated to and by God through your baptism.

"I will sow her for myself in the land. I will also have compassion on her who had not obtained compassion, and I will say to those who were not my people, 'You are my people!' And they will say, 'You are my God!'"
~ Hosea 2:23 (NASB)

https://www.hopetoinspireyou.com/2022/03/22/desert-times/

74

Mount of Temptation

Our next stop is to view the Mount of Temptation, where Jesus was led into the desert for 40 days and nights as Satan tried to tempt Him. This happened right after Jesus was baptized. It is interesting to note that Scripture says "the Spirit" led Jesus into the wilderness or desert.

A monastery at the Mount of Temptation – Jericho, Palestine

Could it be Jesus' temptations were divinely appointed to show us we are not alone when Satan tries to tempt us? We, too, need to follow Jesus' example by using the Word of God to fight Satan. There is power in the Word. Our life mission is to make the Word incarnate real in our lives too. I was overcome with emotion, reflecting on that power while hearing this Scripture:

"Jesus, full of the Holy Spirit, left the Jordan and was led by the Spirit into the wilderness (desert), where for forty days he was tempted by the devil. He ate nothing during those days, and at the end of them he was hungry. The devil said to him, 'If you are the Son of God, tell this stone to become bread.' Jesus answered, 'It is written: "Man shall not live on bread alone."' The devil led him up to a high place and showed him in an instant all the kingdoms of the world. And he said to him, 'I will give you all their authority and splendor; it has been given to me, and I can give it to anyone I want to. If you worship me, it will all be yours.' Jesus answered, 'It is written: "Worship the Lord your God and serve him only."' The devil led him to Jerusalem and had him stand on the highest point of the temple. 'If you are the Son of God,' he said, 'throw yourself down from here. For it is written, "He will command his angels concerning you to guard you carefully; they will lift you up in their hands, so that you will not strike your foot against a stone."' Jesus answered, 'It is said: "Do not put the Lord your God to the test."' When the devil had finished all this tempting, he left him until an opportune time."

~ Luke 4:1-13

REFLECTION:

Do you rely on the Word of God to fight Satan in your life?
Can you see how everything in your life is divinely appointed, both the good times and the bad?

As you reflect on our pilgrimage to Mount Temptation, be encouraged to remember...

to rely on the Word of God when temptations come your way.

"For if you return to the Lord, your brothers and your sons will find compassion in the presence of those who led them captive, and will return

to this land. For the Lord your God is gracious and compassionate, and will not turn his face away from you if you return to him."
~ 2 Chronicles 30:9 (NASB)

https://www.hopetoinspireyou.com/2022/03/22/desert-times/

75

Judean Desert

One of my favorite stops was to the Judean Desert, which is our stop today. Naively, I always envisioned the desert as a flat, sandy area. The Judean Desert was quite the opposite. Beautiful, huge hills and rocky areas enveloped us from all sides. As I stood there, taking in the vast beauty all around, I was thankful I did not have to traverse too far in this desert. I cannot fathom how John the Baptist and Jesus walked this land!

How interesting to read the following verse to realize John the Baptist grew up in the Judean Desert. We know that, like Jesus, John was also around 30 years old when he began his public ministry. It reminds me that God's perfect timing is orchestrated even in the ministries of our lives.

> "And the child (John the Baptist) grew and became strong in spirit; and he lived in the wilderness (desert) until he appeared publicly to Israel."
> ~ Luke 1:80

As some of us pilgrims were walking the hilly path to get closer to the top of the desert spot where we could then view the St. George Monastery, it was a bit scary. I wanted to go closer to the edge of some cliffs where other people were, but I was a little unsure of the rocky, uneven ground. It didn't help that I am afraid of heights.

Standing near me was someone I talked to a few nights earlier, whom I had not known before the pilgrimage. We both felt God's spirit present in our conversation. She, too, was a little unsure of going much further. Her friend, who was in front of her, extended her hand and spoke a word of encouragement to her. That prompted my new friend to be brave and step out further. She, in turn, extended her hand to me, so the three of us were linked. Because of this ripple effect, I was brave enough to journey on to the flatter area and proceed with caution closer to the edge where I wanted to go.

I could not help but think what a perfect lesson I was reminded of in the Judean Desert.

Extending a hand to someone can help that person have more courage to do more than they expected. Great growth can be experienced through a seemingly simple gesture.

My favorite picture of the Judean Desert

REFLECTION:

What are some desert experiences you have had?
Who or what helped you get through the desert?

As you reflect on our pilgrimage to the Judean Desert, be encouraged to remember…

> that God will help you through the desert times of your life.

> *"They refused to listen and failed to remember the miracles you performed among them. They became stiff-necked and in their rebellion appointed a leader in order to return to their slavery. But you are a forgiving God, gracious and compassionate, slow to anger and abounding in love. Therefore you did not desert them."*
> ~ Nehemiah 9:17

https://www.hopetoinspireyou.com/2022/03/22/desert-times/

76

Cana

Hello, my fellow pilgrims. We have arrived in Cana, where Jesus performed His first miracle or sign, as St. John calls them, at a wedding feast. Water has always been a valuable resource. Back in Jesus' day, water was especially important for the Jewish people who often needed to be ceremonially cleansed by pouring water over their hands.

It is interesting to see the significance of Jesus performing His first sign at a wedding feast and how the miracle relates to wine. It symbolizes things about Jesus' mission.

Scripture refers to Christ as the bridegroom, and we, the church, are the bride.

> "As the Scriptures say, 'A man leaves his father and mother and is joined to his wife, and the two are united into one.' This is a great mystery, but it is an illustration of the way Christ and the church are one."
> ~ Ephesians 5:31-32 (NLT)

We know Jesus' blood is the wine, part of the ultimate sacrifice offered for our sins.

> "And he took a cup of wine and gave thanks to God for it. He gave it to them and said, 'Each of you drink from it, for this is my blood, which confirms the covenant between God and his people. It is poured out as a sacrifice to forgive the sins of many.'"
> ~ Matthew 26:27-28 (NLT)

"On the third day a wedding took place at Cana in Galilee. Jesus' mother was there, and Jesus and his disciples had also been invited to the wedding. When the wine was gone, Jesus' mother said to him, 'They have no more wine.' 'Woman, why do you involve me?' Jesus replied. 'My hour has not yet come.' His mother said to the servants, 'Do whatever he tells you.' Nearby stood six stone water jars, the kind used by the Jews for ceremonial washing, each holding from twenty to thirty gallons. Jesus said to the servants, 'Fill the jars with water'; so they filled them to the brim. Then he told them, 'Now draw some out and take it to the master of the banquet.' They did so, and the master of the banquet tasted the water that had been turned into wine. He did not realize where it had come from, though the servants who had drawn the water knew. Then he called the bridegroom aside and said, 'Everyone brings out the choice wine first and then the cheaper wine after the guests have had too much to drink; but you have saved the best till now.' What Jesus did here in Cana of Galilee was the first of the signs through which he revealed his glory; and his disciples believed in him."

~ John 2:1-11

REFLECTION:

In what ways do you recognize and listen to Jesus' voice "doing whatever He tells you?"
How can Jesus turn the water of your life into wine?

While in Cana, we saw a few rooms of a house back in Jesus' day. It was hard to fathom how families could live in such small areas. As I listened to the tour guide, what struck me was the timelessness of God's Word. Our world these days is so different between technology and the luxuries we have, yet God's Word is just as applicable to our lives. How amazing is that to reflect on?

Small rooms!

As you reflect on our pilgrimage to Cana, be encouraged to remember to…

do whatever He tells you.

"I will show you compassion so that he will have compassion on you and restore you to your land."
~ Jeremiah 42:12

https://www.hopetoinspireyou.com/2022/03/29/public-ministry/

77

Capernaum

SYNOGOGUE – BREAD OF LIFE DISCOURSE

Here we are in Capernaum, where Jesus' public ministry began. It was the village that became the adopted home of Jesus after He left Nazareth.

> *"He went first to Nazareth, then left there and moved to Capernaum, beside the Sea of Galilee, in the region of Zebulun and Naphtali."*
> ~ Matthew 4:13 (NLT)

Jesus taught in the synagogue here. It was also where He healed the paralytic, the man with the withered hand, and the centurion's servant, to name a few of Jesus' miracles.

I was overcome with emotion while standing at this synagogue, listening to the following Scripture, knowing this was where Jesus spoke. It was a sacred encounter with Jesus that was a definite highlight, and I did not want to leave.

The Synagogue where Jesus gave the Bread of Life Discourse

"Do not work for food that spoils, but for food that endures to eternal life, which the Son of Man will give you. For on him God the Father has placed his seal of approval.' Jesus said to them, 'Very truly I tell you, it is not Moses who has given you the bread from heaven, but it is my Father who gives you the true bread from heaven. For the bread of God is the bread that comes down from heaven and gives life to the world.' 'Sir,' they said, 'always give us this bread.' Then Jesus declared, 'I am the bread of life. Whoever comes to me will never go hungry, and whoever believes in me will never be thirsty.' Just as the living Father sent me and I live because of the Father, so the one who feeds on me will live because of me. He said this while teaching in the synagogue in Capernaum."
~ John 6:27, 32-35, 57, 59

REFLECTION:

Do you work for food that endures for all eternity?
Is your heart filled with the One who provides the bread of life and the wine to satisfy your thirst?

Peter's House

Right next to this synagogue is Peter's house, where the following Scripture took place. Many of the sites we visit have churches built over them to help preserve the areas.

*"When Jesus arrived at Peter's house,
Peter's mother-in-law was sick in bed with a high fever.
But when Jesus touched her hand, the fever left her.
Then she got up and prepared a meal for him."*
~ Matthew 8:14-15 (NLT)

REFLECTION:

Do you reach for Jesus' hand in your time of need?
In what ways do you try to keep growing in your faith journey?

At Peter's house, I went outside my comfort zone because I wanted to be bold enough to proclaim Scripture in the Holy Land. I was in the right place at the right time. I am grateful for the privilege and that the acoustics were good as there was no microphone.

As you reflect on our pilgrimage to Capernaum this week, be encouraged to remember to…

> be filled with food and drink from Jesus.
> reach for Jesus in your time of need.

> *"Now Jesus called his disciples to him and said, 'I feel compassion for the people, because they have remained with me now for three days and have nothing to eat; and I do not want to send them away hungry, for they might faint on the way.'"*
> ~ Matthew 15:32 (NASB)

https://www.hopetoinspireyou.com/2022/03/29/public-ministry/

78

Sea of Galilee

Our next stop is the Sea of Galilee where Jesus spent a lot of time going to different towns to preach and heal many people. We had the full experience of a stormy sea, as it was raining and windy during our time on the Sea of Galilee. Our boat succumbed to the big crests of water. It was quite challenging to dock the boat as it took four attempts.

Come aboard for our boat ride on the Sea of Galilee!

The boat ride on the Sea of Galilee was another highlight of the pilgrimage. I spent most of my time in solitude at the front of the boat, holding on, embracing the wind, and enjoying a better view. It was an amazing experience to be on a boat on the Sea of Galilee, knowing Jesus was here many times. I was looking at the same mountains and places as He did.

I like how this Scripture teaches us that Jesus is not only Lord of us, but of nature too. God is more powerful than the storms in our lives.

Enjoy the ride seeing what Jesus saw!

"Then he got into the boat and his disciples followed him. Suddenly a furious storm came up on the lake, so that the waves swept over the boat. But Jesus was sleeping. The disciples went and woke him, saying, 'Lord, save us! We're going to drown!' He replied, 'You of little faith, why are you so afraid?' Then he got up and rebuked the winds and the waves, and it was completely calm. The men were amazed and asked, 'What kind of man is this? Even the winds and the waves obey him!'"
~ Matthew 8:23-27

REFLECTION:

Do you reach out in faith to Jesus when the waters of life get rough? How is Jesus the peace in your life when the water of storms overwhelms you?

As you reflect on our pilgrimage stop at the Sea of Galilee, be encouraged to remember to...

> not be afraid as Jesus is in control of everything in this life.

"I will tell of the kindnesses of the Lord, the deeds for which he is to be praised, according to all the Lord has done for us— yes, the many good things he has done for Israel, according to his compassion and many kindnesses."
~ Isaiah 63:7

https://www.hopetoinspireyou.com/2022/03/29/public-ministry/

79

Mount of Beatitudes

Eremos Cave at the bottom of the Mount of Beatitudes, where Jesus is believed to have prayed and gotten away from the crowd

Hello, my fellow pilgrims. Today we are at the Mount of Beatitudes area. For our time in Galilee, we stayed at a guesthouse there. Walking the grounds we saw the beautiful landscape of the area, the Sea of Galilee, and the Mount of Beatitudes church.

As our tour guide read and explained the Beatitudes Scripture, I gained new insights. There is an interesting parallel to thinking about how Moses received the Ten Commandments, the law, from God on Mount Sinai. Here, on the Mount of Beatitudes, Jesus brought us the Beatitudes, a message of the Law of Love. Jesus came to fulfill the law, the Law of Love.

"Now when Jesus saw the crowds, he went up on a mountainside and sat down.

> *His disciples came to him and he began to teach them.*
> *He said:*
> *'Blessed are the poor in spirit,*
> *for theirs is the kingdom of heaven.*
> *Blessed are those who mourn,*
> *for they will be comforted.*
> *Blessed are the meek,*
> *for they will inherit the earth.*
> *Blessed are those who hunger and thirst for righteousness,*
> *for they will be filled.*
> *Blessed are the merciful,*
> *for they will be shown mercy.*
> *Blessed are the pure in heart,*
> *for they will see God.*
> *Blessed are the peacemakers,*
> *for they will be called children of God.*
> *Blessed are those who are persecuted because of righteousness,*
> *for theirs is the kingdom of heaven.*
> *Blessed are you when people insult you, persecute you and falsely say all kinds of evil against you because of me. Rejoice and be glad, because great is your reward in heaven, for in the same way they persecuted the prophets who were before you.'*
> ~ Matthew 5:1-12

The word blessed can be translated as happy. I never noticed how the Beatitudes build on each other, kind of like climbing a ladder. As you read, consider the blessing we receive with the second half of each of the Beatitudes.

Being poor in spirit can mean spiritual poverty where we recognize we need God's help. We surrender our lives and ourselves to God. This spiritual poverty leads our hearts to be sensitive to the needs, pain, and losses of others, joining in their mourning. We also mourn our own weaknesses, the way we sin, or fail to love unconditionally. This leads to the next Beatitude of being meek. Meekness, in the biblical sense, means we align our will with God's will. We follow Christ no matter what the risk or what others think. When we hunger and thirst for righteousness, we desperately crave Christ. We have a deep desire to continually feed upon the Word, spend time with Him, and share His love and goodness with others.

This next rung of our ladder is the Beatitude of being merciful. Being merciful is self-giving, forgiving with the forgiveness God has granted to us, and loving our enemies, even those who persecute us. The next rung leads to being pure in heart. Our hearts are the center of God's activity in us. Scripture tells us our hearts are the center of the human spirit, from which spring emotions, thoughts, motivations, courage, and action. Being pure in heart leads us to be peacemakers. Peacemakers share healing in words and actions, keeping in mind that we are all made in God's image. We are all valuable in God's kingdom. Some of us, through the ages, have faced persecution for our faith. Maybe loved ones have deserted us because of our faith. We are joined in carrying the cross of Jesus. Our reward in heaven, too, will be great!

REFLECTION:

When have you experienced God's presence, once far away, become close to you in your suffering?
Do you need to work on a particular rung of the ladder of the Beatitudes?

In awe of sitting in a cave where Jesus did!

The view from the cave overlooking the Sea of Galilee

As you reflect on our pilgrimage stop at the Mount of Beatitudes, be encouraged to remember to...

live out the ladder of the Beatitudes daily.

"Therefore, I urge you, brothers and sisters, in view of God's mercy, to offer your bodies as a living sacrifice, holy and pleasing to God— this is your true and proper worship."
~ Romans 12:1

https://www.hopetoinspireyou.com/2022/04/05/last-day-in-galilee/

80

Tabgha

Our next stop is to the village of Tabgha, where Jesus' miracle of feeding the five thousand took place. It is a story told by all four gospel writers. In retrospect, I realize the sacredness of standing in the place known as the Church of the Multiplication, where Jesus performed this miracle, did not hit me. What a privilege it is to be standing here. A highlight of the church here is seeing the restored fifth-century mosaic floor.

> *"When Jesus heard what had happened, he withdrew by boat privately to a solitary place. Hearing of this, the crowds followed him on foot from the towns. When Jesus landed and saw a large crowd, he had compassion on them and healed their sick. As evening approached, the disciples came to him and said, 'This is a remote place, and it's already getting late. Send the crowds away, so they can go to the villages and buy themselves some food.' Jesus replied, 'They do not need to go away. You give them something to eat.' 'We have here only five loaves of bread and two fish,' they answered. 'Bring them here to me,' he said. And he directed the people to sit down on the grass. Taking the five loaves and the two fish and looking up to heaven, he gave thanks and broke the loaves. Then he gave them to the disciples, and the disciples gave them to the people. They all ate and were satisfied, and the disciples picked up twelve basketfuls of broken pieces that were left over. The number of those who ate was about five thousand men, besides women and children."*
> ~ Matthew 14:13-21

REFLECTION:

Do you offer Jesus the little you have, generously and unashamedly, so He can turn it into something greater for His glory?
Do you give thanks to God for your life and ask Him to use you to bless others?

As you reflect on our pilgrimage stop at Tabgha, be encouraged to remember to…

> daily offer Jesus the little you have so He can multiply it for His glory.

"When he saw the crowds, he had compassion on them because they were confused and helpless, like sheep without a shepherd."
~ Matthew 9:36 (NLT)

https://www.hopetoinspireyou.com/2022/04/05/last-day-in-galilee/

81

Magdala

MAGDALA

We have arrived in Magdala, the village where Mary Magdalene, one of Jesus' loyal followers, lived. It was a well-known fishing town along the Sea of Galilee. A first-century synagogue, known as the Magdala Synagogue, was unearthed here along with the Magdala Stone in 2009. The Magdala Stone is a carved stone block replica, which dates to before the destruction of the Second Temple in Jerusalem in the year 70. There is a carving of a menorah and some coins.

The Sea of Galilee in Magdala, a fishing town back in Jesus' day

"One day as Jesus was standing by the Lake of Gennesaret, the people were crowding around him and listening to the word of God. He saw at the water's edge two boats, left there by the fishermen, who were

washing their nets. He got into one of the boats, the one belonging to Simon, and asked him to put out a little from shore. Then he sat down and taught the people from the boat. When he had finished speaking, he said to Simon, 'Put out into deep water, and let down the nets for a catch.' Simon answered, 'Master, we've worked hard all night and haven't caught anything. But because you say so, I will let down the nets.' When they had done so, they caught such a large number of fish that their nets began to break. So they signaled their partners in the other boat to come and help them, and they came and filled both boats so full that they began to sink. When Simon Peter saw this, he fell at Jesus' knees and said, 'Go away from me, Lord; I am a sinful man!' For he and all his companions were astonished at the catch of fish they had taken, and so were James and John, the sons of Zebedee, Simon's partners. Then Jesus said to Simon, 'Don't be afraid; from now on you will fish for people.' So they pulled their boats up on shore, left everything and followed him."
~ Luke 5:1-11

REFLECTION:

Do you put your net into the deep water following Jesus' lead, even when it seems impractical?
How do you fish for people in your life, bringing them into a relationship with Jesus?

SYNAGOGUE

It was surreal to stand in this place that has original stones from a synagogue where Jesus preached.

A stone bench from a synagogue back in Jesus' day

Seeing this beautiful, realistic painting of the woman with the issue of blood touching the hem of Jesus' garment as He was passing by, was a God moment. The tour guide suggested we reach out to touch the hem of Jesus' garment as we prayed for people who needed a miracle in their lives.

Touching the hem of Jesus' garment, lifting friends in prayer

"And a woman was there who had been subject to bleeding for twelve years, but no one could heal her. She came up behind him and touched the edge of his cloak, and immediately her bleeding stopped. 'Who touched me?' Jesus asked. When they all denied it, Peter said, 'Master, the people are crowding and pressing against you.' But Jesus said, 'Someone touched me; I know that power has gone out from me.' Then the woman, seeing that she could not go unnoticed, came trembling and fell at his feet. In the presence of all the people, she told why she had touched him and how she had been instantly healed. Then he said to her, 'Daughter, your faith has healed you. Go in peace.'"
~ Luke 8:43-48

REFLECTION:

Do you reach out to touch the hem of Jesus' cloak?
What healing power has Jesus demonstrated for you?

As you reflect on our pilgrimage stop at Magdala, be encouraged to remember to...

> let the net of your life down in deep water, letting Jesus guide you.
> reach out in faith and touch the hem of Jesus' garment.

"If you take your neighbor's cloak as a pledge, return it by sunset, because that cloak is the only covering your neighbor has. What else can they sleep in? When they cry out to me, I will hear, for I am compassionate."
~ Exodus 22:26-27

https://www.hopetoinspireyou.com/2022/04/05/last-day-in-galilee/

82

Bethsaida

Our last stop to complete our time in Galilee is Bethsaida, the birthplace of the disciples Peter, Andrew, and Philip. We were able to visit an archeological site where we saw parts of the walled city that one of our tour hosts assisted on some years ago. Jesus also performed miracles in Bethsaida, one of which was a little different. For one blind man, Jesus' healing was not immediate; rather, it was in two stages, something to reflect on. Isn't that like us in coming to faith? Doesn't faith, too, come in stages in our lives and continue to grow?

> *"They came to Bethsaida, and some people brought a blind man and begged Jesus to touch him. He took the blind man by the hand and led him outside the village. When he had spit on the man's eyes and put his hands on him, Jesus asked, 'Do you see anything?' He looked up and said, 'I see people; they look like trees walking around.' Once more Jesus put his hands on the man's eyes. Then his eyes were opened, his sight was restored, and he saw everything clearly."*
> ~ Mark 8:22-25

REFLECTION:

Do you need Jesus to heal the spiritual blindness of your heart?
Are the eyes of your heart open to Jesus working in your life?

As you reflect on our pilgrimage stop at Bethsaida, be encouraged to remember to…

keep striving to grow in your faith journey, especially seeing with the eyes of your heart.

"Is not Ephraim my dear son, the child in whom I delight?
Though I often speak against him, I still remember him.
Therefore my heart yearns for him;
I have great compassion for him," declares the Lord."
~ Jeremiah 31:20

https://www.hopetoinspireyou.com/2022/04/05/last-day-in-galilee/

83

Dominus Flevit and Upper Room

Hello, my fellow pilgrims. We journey south to Jerusalem today as we begin to walk in Jesus' footsteps of His passion and death. You can see the view of the city of Jerusalem that Jesus saw as He approached the city on the first Palm Sunday.

DOMINUS FLEVIT

We have a quick stop at the chapel called Dominus Flevit, which means "The Lord Wept," located on the Mount of Olives. The Lord wept over Jerusalem because it failed to recognize the peace that comes from knowing who Jesus was. They were blinded to the knowledge that God was present with them through the person of Jesus.

Dominus Flevit on the Mount of Olives overlooking Jerusalem

"As he approached Jerusalem and saw the city, he wept over it and said, 'If you, even you, had only known on this day what would bring you

peace— but now it is hidden from your eyes. The days will come upon you when your enemies will build an embankment against you and encircle you and hem you in on every side. They will dash you to the ground, you and the children within your walls. They will not leave one stone on another, because you did not recognize the time of God's coming to you.'"
~ Luke 19:41-44

REFLECTION:

Have you wept for your loved ones who do not know the peace Christ gives?
Was there a time in your life you failed to recognize God's presence?

As you reflect on our pilgrimage stop to Dominus Flevit, be encouraged to remember to…

> seek the things in life that bring peace to your spirit.

"'Therefore this is what the Sovereign Lord says: I will now restore the fortunes of Jacob and will have compassion on all the people of Israel, and I will be zealous for my holy name.'"
~ Ezekiel 39:25

https://www.hopetoinspireyou.com/2022/04/12/holy-week-in-jerusalem/

UPPER ROOM

We travel next to the place believed to have been in the area of the Upper Room where Jesus celebrated the Last Supper with His disciples on Holy Thursday. This is located in the oldest part of Jerusalem, known as the City of David or the City of Zion. It is also the location where the first Christian community gathered after Pentecost.

I find the Holy Thursday passages meaningful because of Jesus' washing His disciples' feet and celebrating the Eucharist with them. Jesus, King of the Jews, was a true humble servant in showing us that we are all equals. None of us should think we are better than others. Take special note of the last sentence in the following Scripture. Jesus tells His disciples and us how we need to put our knowledge and love into action. We are to follow Jesus' example.

The Golden Olive Tree in The Upper Room at The Last Supper Cenacle

"So he got up from the table, took off his robe, wrapped a towel around his waist, and poured water into a basin. Then he began to wash the disciples' feet, drying them with the towel he had around him. After washing their feet, he put on his robe again and sat down and asked, 'Do you understand what I was doing? You call me "Teacher" and "Lord," and you are right, because that's what I am. And since I, your Lord and Teacher, have washed your feet, you ought to wash each other's

feet. I have given you an example to follow. Do as I have done to you. I tell you the truth, slaves are not greater than their master. Nor is the messenger more important than the one who sends the message. Now that you know these things, God will bless you for doing them.'"
~ John 13:4-5, 12-17 (NLT)

REFLECTION:

Do you live the humble life of a servant knowing you are equal with all of God's children?
Are you challenged to put into action your knowledge of Christ's examples of being a disciple?

As you reflect on our pilgrimage stop to the Upper Room area, be encouraged to remember to...

>put Christ's servant examples into action.

"And he remembered his covenant for their sake, and relented according to the greatness of his mercy. He also made them objects of compassion in the presence of all their captors."
~ Psalm 106:45-46 (NASB)

https://www.hopetoinspireyou.com/2022/04/12/holy-week-in-jerusalem/

Garden of Gethsemane

Overlooking the Garden of Gethsemane, holding an olive branch

We are on the road again. We have arrived at the Garden of Gethsemane, one place I was excited to see. I failed to think there would be a fence around the actual garden, so we could not walk through it. Next to the garden is a church that contains the rock where Jesus cried out to God in the following Scripture. It was a sacred moment to be praying at the rock where Jesus agonized in prayer.

We were fortunate to find freshly cut olive branches we were able to take home. It was interesting to gaze upon these massive olive trees and to think of the parallels to what Jesus was going to endure in the next few days. Just as olives are picked, crushed, and pressed to make oil, Jesus would experience those same things in His life to set us free from our sins.

Olive trees

"They went to a place called Gethsemane, and Jesus said to his disciples, 'Sit here while I pray.' He took Peter, James and John along with him, and he began to be deeply distressed and troubled. 'My soul is overwhelmed with sorrow to the point of death,' he said to them. 'Stay here and keep watch.' Going a little farther, he fell to the ground and prayed that if possible the hour might pass from him. 'Abba, Father,' he said, 'everything is possible for you. Take this cup from me. Yet not what I will, but what you will.'"
~ Mark 14:32-36

REFLECTION:

When you are walking through overwhelming times in life, do you share your feelings and pain with God?
Eventually, are you able to say, "God, not what I will, but Your will be done?"

As you reflect on our pilgrimage stop to the Garden of Gethsemane, remember to pray...

"Let Your will be done, God."

"But the Lord was gracious to them and had compassion and showed concern for them because of his covenant with Abraham, Isaac and Jacob. To this day he has been unwilling to destroy them or banish them from his presence."
~ 2 Kings 13:23

https://www.hopetoinspireyou.com/2022/04/12/holy-week-in-jerusalem/

85

St Peter of Gallicantu

ST. PETER OF GALLICANTU

Our next destination is the Church of Saint Peter in Gallincantu (a Latin word meaning cock's-crow) on Mount Zion. It commemorates the place where Peter denied knowing Jesus three times, his repentance, and reconciliation with Jesus.

> *"Then seizing him, they led him away and took him into the house of the high priest. Peter followed at a distance. And when some there had kindled a fire in the middle of the courtyard and had sat down together, Peter sat down with them. A servant girl saw him seated there in the firelight. She looked closely at him and said, 'This man was with him.' But he denied it. 'Woman, I don't know him,' he said. A little later someone else saw him and said, 'You also are one of them.' 'Man, I am not!' Peter replied. About an hour later another asserted, 'Certainly this fellow was with him, for he is a Galilean.' Peter replied, 'Man, I don't know what you're talking about!' Just as he was speaking, the rooster crowed. The Lord turned and looked straight at Peter. Then Peter remembered the word the Lord had spoken to him: 'Before the rooster crows today, you will disown me three times' And he went outside and wept bitterly."*
> ~ Luke 22:54-62

REFLECTION:

In what ways do you deny knowing Jesus in your life?
Do you see Jesus looking at you and seeing the forgiveness in His eyes, knowing His love is unconditional?

THE DUNGEON

This spot is also believed to be the location of the palace of High Priest Caiaphas. It was a special experience to be sitting alone, in solitude, in the dungeon that is believed to be the cell where Jesus was detained the night of His arrest at the Garden of Gethsemane. We read Psalm 88, which very well could be the thoughts of Jesus. It is the only Psalm that does not leave you encouraged.

> *"Lord, you are the God who saves me;*
> *day and night I cry out to you.*
> *May my prayer come before you;*
> *turn your ear to my cry.*
> *I am overwhelmed with troubles*
> *and my life draws near to death.*
> *I am counted among those who go down to the pit;*
> *I am like one without strength.*
> *I am set apart with the dead,*
> *like the slain who lie in the grave,*
> *whom you remember no more,*
> *who are cut off from your care.*
>
> *You have put me in the lowest pit,*
> *in the darkest depths.*
> *Your wrath lies heavily on me;*
> *you have overwhelmed me with all your waves.*
> *You have taken from me my closest friends*
> *and have made me repulsive to them.*
> *I am confined and cannot escape;*
> *my eyes are dim with grief.*

I call to you, Lord, every day;
I spread out my hands to you.
Do you show your wonders to the dead?
Do their spirits rise up and praise you?
Is your love declared in the grave,
your faithfulness in Destruction?
Are your wonders known in the place of darkness,
or your righteous deeds in the land of oblivion?

But I cry to you for help, Lord;
in the morning my prayer comes before you.
Why, Lord, do you reject me
and hide your face from me?

From my youth I have suffered and been close to death;
I have borne your terrors and am in despair.
Your wrath has swept over me;
your terrors have destroyed me.
All day long they surround me like a flood;
they have completely engulfed me.
You have taken from me friend and neighbor—
darkness is my closest friend."
~ Psalm 88:1-18

REFLECTION:

When were you in the lowest pit of your life?
Do you keep calling out to the Lord in your distress, knowing He is caring for you?

Sitting alone in the dungeon, I was thinking of Jesus sitting there, and I imagined Him saying this to me:

The Dark Night

Stone cold
No food
All alone in the dark dungeon
Enduring separation
Beatings to set you free!
Yes, I endured for you, my friend
I love you this much.

Solitude–loneliness
Separation
Doing the will of my Father
I was tortured to set you free.

Release your fear and anxiety
I came to set you free–
Free from sin and bondage
I took your sins upon me
So you don't have to.

Peace, I have come to bring you
Peace no matter what happens in your life.

Christine M. Fisher

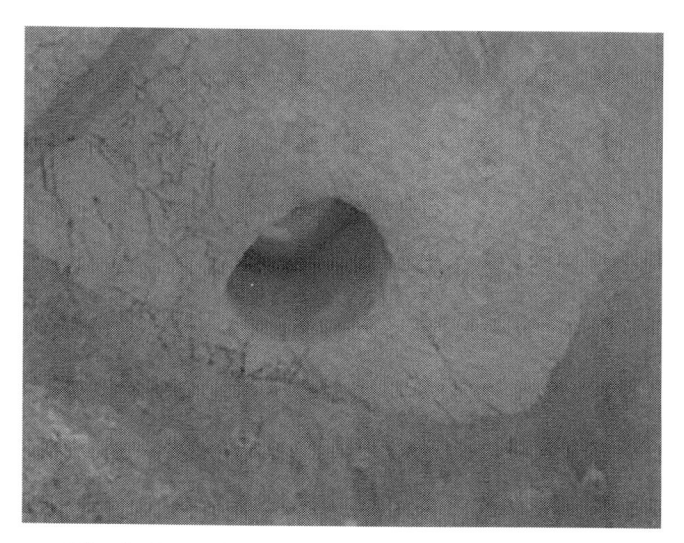

The hole in the ceiling where they would have lowered Jesus into the dungeon

The small dungeon space where Jesus was detained overnight

From Scripture, we know Jesus was then handed over to the Roman governor, Pilate. Jesus, an innocent man, endured an agonizing Roman crucifixion. He was first bound and then took on His body, 121 lashings. Seeing the place where Jesus was tortured, and the tools used to whip and beat Him was difficult.

Where Jesus was bound and whipped

As you reflect on our pilgrimage stop to St. Peter of Gallicantu, be encouraged to remember to...

> experience God's unconditional love for you.
> cry out to God in your distress.

> *"Once again you will have compassion on us.*
> *You will trample our sins under your feet and*
> *throw them into the depths of the ocean!"*
> ~ Micah 7:19 (NLT)

https://www.hopetoinspireyou.com/2022/04/12/holy-week-in-jerusalem/

86

Holy Sepulchre

Our stop today is at the Holy Sepulchre, the church that contains the two holiest sites in Christianity. One is Golgotha, also called Calvary, where Jesus was crucified, and the other is the tomb where He was buried and resurrected. It was a little harder to visualize what the places were like when Jesus was there, as they are located inside. It was powerful, nonetheless.

The entrance of the Holy Sepulchre

At Calvary, you can kneel and put your arm in the hole where Jesus' cross was. Next to it, you see the Rock of Calvary. I had the honor of proclaiming Scripture in the Golgotha Chapel right near the site.

Touching the place where Jesus hung on the cross

The Rock of Calvary

Christine M. Fisher

Proclaiming Scripture at Golgotha Chapel

"Carrying his own cross, he went out to the place of the Skull (which in Aramaic is called Golgotha). There they crucified him, and with him two others— one on each side and Jesus in the middle."
~ John 19:17-18

"When he had received the drink, Jesus said, 'It is finished.' With that, he bowed his head and gave up his spirit."
~ John 19:30

There are two little rooms where Jesus' tomb is. The first is called the Angel's Stone, which encases a piece of the stone that sealed Jesus' tomb. The second room contains Jesus' tomb. What a privilege it was to be able to touch Jesus' tomb.

The outside of Jesus' tomb area

Touching Jesus' tomb

Right inside the entrance of the Holy Sepulchre, there is the Stone of Anointing, which has a lovely scent of roses. This is the place where Jesus' body was laid after being removed from the crucifix and prepared for burial. It is also the spot where Mary, Jesus' mother, and John, Jesus' disciple charged with taking care of Mary, would have been standing watching Jesus take His last breath.

The Stone of Anointing

"Taking Jesus' body, the two of them wrapped it, with the spices, in strips of linen. This was in accordance with Jewish burial customs. At the place where Jesus was crucified, there was a garden, and in the garden a new tomb, in which no one had ever been laid. Because it was the Jewish day of Preparation and since the tomb was nearby, they laid Jesus there."
~ John 19:40-42

After my pilgrimage to the Holy Land, I researched and read more books about the sites and realized the significance of standing in the place where Jesus rose from the dead. That is the spot where the centrality of our faith occurred. What gratitude fills my heart.

> "Now Mary stood outside the tomb crying. As she wept, she bent over to look into the tomb and saw two angels in white, seated where Jesus' body had been, one at the head and the other at the foot. They asked her, 'Woman, why are you crying?' 'They have taken my Lord away,' she said, 'and I don't know where they have put him.' At this, she turned around and saw Jesus standing there, but she did not realize that it was Jesus. He asked her, 'Woman, why are you crying? Who is it you are looking for?' Thinking he was the gardener, she said, 'Sir, if you have carried him away, tell me where you have put him, and I will get him.' Jesus said to her, 'Mary.' She turned toward him and cried out in Aramaic, 'Rabboni!' (which means "Teacher"). Jesus said, 'Do not hold on to me, for I have not yet ascended to the Father. Go instead to my brothers and tell them, "I am ascending to my Father and your Father, to my God and your God." Mary Magdalene went to the disciples with the news: 'I have seen the Lord!' And she told them that he had said these things to her."
> ~ John 20:11-18

REFLECTION:

How do you share in carrying Jesus' cross?
In what ways do you see the Risen Christ daily in your life?

As you reflect on our pilgrimage stop at the Holy Sepulchre, be encouraged to remember to…

> let the Risen Christ shine in your life.

> "He saved us, not because of righteous things we had done, but because of his mercy. He saved us through the washing rebirth and renewal by the Holy Spirit."
> ~ Titus 3:5

https://www.hopetoinspireyou.com/2022/04/12/holy-week-in-jerusalem/

87

Church of the Resurrection

We ended yesterday by hearing Mary Magdalene, the first person who saw the Risen Christ, proclaim: *"I have seen the Lord!"* Come experience a couple more sightings of the Risen Jesus.

Today we stop at the Church of the Resurrection in Abu Ghosh, one of four possible sites believed to have been referenced in the Bible story, "On the Road to Emmaus." The exact location became lost in the early Christian era and was made more difficult by conflicting distance calculations mentioned in Luke's Gospel. This is a 12th-century, echo-like-sounding church that has wall and ceiling paintings (frescoes) remaining from the Crusaders. There are no faces on the people in the paintings. The Muslims who took over the region had a strict rule of depicting no images of humans in their art. It was seen as a violation of the commandment to not make any graven images.

"Now that same day two of them were going to a village called Emmaus, about seven miles from Jerusalem. They were talking with each other about everything that had happened. As they talked and discussed these things with each other, Jesus himself came up and walked along with them; but they were kept from recognizing him He asked them, 'What are you discussing together as you walk along?' They stood still, their faces downcast. One of them, named Cleopas, asked him, 'Are you the only one visiting Jerusalem who does not know the things that have happened there in these days?' 'What things?' he asked. 'About Jesus of Nazareth,' they replied. 'He was a prophet, powerful in word and deed before God and all the people. The chief priests and our rulers handed him over to be sentenced to death, and

they crucified him; but we had hoped that he was the one who was going to redeem Israel. And what is more, it is the third day since all this took place. In addition, some of our women amazed us. They went to the tomb early this morning but didn't find his body. They came and told us that they had seen a vision of angels, who said he was alive. Then some of our companions went to the tomb and found it just as the women had said, but they did not see Jesus.' He said to them, 'How foolish you are, and how slow to believe all that the prophets have spoken! Did not the Messiah have to suffer these things and then enter his glory?' And beginning with Moses and all the Prophets, he explained to them what was said in all the Scriptures concerning himself. As they approached the village to which they were going, Jesus continued on as if he were going farther. But they urged him strongly, 'Stay with us, for it is nearly evening; the day is almost over.' So he went in to stay with them. When he was at the table with them, he took bread, gave thanks, broke it and began to give it to them. Then their eyes were opened and they recognized him, and he disappeared from their sight. They asked each other, 'Were not our hearts burning within us while he talked with us on the road and opened the Scriptures to us?'"

~ Luke 24:13-32

REFLECTION:

Do you hear Jesus asking you why you are downcast and recognize how He listens when you share?
Is your heart filled with joy when you recognize Jesus in the breaking of bread, the Scriptures, and the everyday events?

As you reflect on our pilgrimage stop today, be encouraged to remember to…

talk with Jesus about everything; He is always listening.

"Praise be to the God and Father of our Lord Jesus Christ! In his great mercy he has given us new birth into a living hope through the resurrection of Jesus Christ from the dead."
~ 1 Peter 1:3

https://www.hopetoinspireyou.com/2022/04/19/resurrection-appearances/

88

Primacy of St Peter

The Rock Where Jesus Served Bread and Fish

We journey now to the Church of the Primacy of St. Peter/Mensa Christi in Tabgha, located on the northwest shore of the Sea of Galilee. Mensa Christi means "table of Christ." This is believed to be the third spot where the Risen Jesus appeared to the disciples. Jesus saw the disciples fishing with no success and told them where to put their net. Then He prepared breakfast and ate with them.

The rock where Jesus served the disciples the bread and fish for breakfast

"Afterward Jesus appeared again to his disciples, by the Sea of Galilee. It happened this way: Simon Peter, Thomas (also known as Didymus), Nathanael from Cana in Galilee, the sons of Zebedee, and two other disciples

were together. 'I'm going out to fish,' Simon Peter told them, and they said, 'We'll go with you.' So they went out and got into the boat, but that night they caught nothing. Early in the morning, Jesus stood on the shore, but the disciples did not realize that it was Jesus. He called out to them, 'Friends, haven't you any fish?' 'No,' they answered. He said, 'Throw your net on the right side of the boat and you will find some.' When they did, they were unable to haul the net in because of the large number of fish. Then the disciple whom Jesus loved said to Peter, 'It is the Lord!' As soon as Simon Peter heard him say, 'It is the Lord,' he wrapped his outer garment around him (for he had taken it off) and jumped into the water. The other disciples followed in the boat, towing the net full of fish, for they were not far from shore, about a hundred yards. When they landed, they saw a fire of burning coals there with fish on it, and some bread. Jesus said to them, 'Bring some of the fish you have just caught.' So Simon Peter climbed back into the boat and dragged the net ashore. It was full of large fish, 153, but even with so many the net was not torn. Jesus said to them, 'Come and have breakfast.' None of the disciples dared ask him, 'Who are you?' They knew it was the Lord. Jesus came, took the bread and gave it to them, and did the same with the fish. This was now the third time Jesus appeared to his disciples after he was raised from the dead."

~ John 21:1-14

REFLECTION:

Do you try to walk in obedience to the Lord and see the fruitfulness it produces in your life?

In what ways do you experience the Lord calling you to commune with Him throughout the day?

JESUS FORGIVES SIMON PETER

Continuing in Scripture, we see where Jesus focused His attention on Simon Peter, who denied Him three times and wept bitterly after realizing what he had done. What a wonderful story of the forgiveness Jesus extended to a penitent Peter. There is a powerful encounter where Jesus asked Peter three times if he loved Him, to counter the three times Peter denied Him. I believe Jesus is testing Peter's heart. Peter declared his love and faith in Christ and was rewarded for it. Jesus commanded Peter to take care of and feed the lambs and sheep, the church that Jesus was leaving to him because of Peter's profession of who Jesus is.

> "When they had finished eating, Jesus said to Simon Peter, 'Simon son of John, do you love me more than these?' 'Yes, Lord,' he said, 'you know that I love you.' Jesus said, 'Feed my lambs.' Again Jesus said, 'Simon son of John, do you love me?' He answered, 'Yes, Lord, you know that I love you.' Jesus said, 'Take care of my sheep.' The third time he said to him, 'Simon son of John, do you love me?' Peter was hurt because Jesus asked him the third time, 'Do you love me?' He said, 'Lord, you know all things; you know that I love you.' Jesus said, 'Feed my sheep. Very truly I tell you, when you were younger you dressed yourself and went where you wanted; but when you are old you will stretch out your hands, and someone else will dress you and lead you where you do not want to go.' Jesus said this to indicate the kind of death by which Peter would glorify God. Then he said to him, 'Follow me!'"
> ~ John 21:15-19

REFLECTION:

Do you love Jesus with the highest form of love, agape love?
In what ways do you take care of and feed Jesus' flock?

EYEWITNESSES WHO SAW JESUS AFTER THE RESURRECTION

From the reality of Jesus' resurrection, we know that Jesus indeed walked this earth and was also divine. Many eyewitnesses can attest to this truth. To further validate the resurrection, consider how no one has ever unearthed or found any bones or the skeleton of Jesus through these 2000 years. Recently, that thought struck me, making Jesus more personal.

What a powerful message Paul shares with the following Scripture. Let these words touch your soul.

> *"I passed on to you what was most important and what had also been passed on to me. Christ died for our sins, just as the Scriptures said. He was buried, and he was raised from the dead on the third day, just as the Scriptures said. He was seen by Peter and then by the Twelve. After that, he was seen by more than 500 of his followers at one time, most of whom are still alive, though some have died. Then he was seen by James and later by all the apostles. Last of all, as though I had been born at the wrong time, I also saw him. For I am the least of all the apostles. In fact, I'm not even worthy to be called an apostle after the way I persecuted God's church."*
> ~ 1 Corinthians 15:3-9 (NLT)

REFLECTION:

In what ways do you pass on the good news of Christ's life, death, and resurrection?

Even though you were born 2000 years after Jesus, how do you see the Risen Jesus in your life?

The Ascension Into Heaven

To complete our travels in the footsteps of Jesus, we must mention the site of His ascension into heaven, which was forty days after His resurrection. We did not travel to the specific site, but we could see the spot that commemorates it while in Jerusalem. It is called Chapel of the Ascension, which is located on the Mount of Olives in Jerusalem. Jesus told His disciples they would receive power through the Holy Spirit to be His witnesses, even to the ends of the earth.

We are privileged to have that same Holy Spirit power in our lives as well.

Keep witnessing for Jesus, even to the ends of the earth, my dear reader.

"After his suffering, he presented himself to them and gave many convincing proofs that he was alive. He appeared to them over a period of forty days and spoke about the kingdom of God. Then they gathered around him and asked him, "Lord, are you at this time going to restore the kingdom to Israel?" He said to them: "It is not for you to know the times or dates the Father has set by his own authority. But you will receive power when the Holy Spirit comes on you; and you will be my witnesses in Jerusalem, and in all Judea and Samaria, and to the ends of the earth." After he said this, he was taken up before their very eyes, and a cloud hid him from their sight."
~ Acts 1:3, 6-9

REFLECTION:

In what ways do you experience the Holy Spirit's power?
How does your life witness to the Spirit in you?

As you reflect on our pilgrimage stops today, be encouraged to remember to…

>be obedient to Jesus leading you.
>love Jesus with the agape love He loves you with.
>share the Risen Jesus using the gifts He has given you.
>let the Holy Spirit's power bear witness in you to the ends of the earth.

>*"You, Lord, will not withhold your compassion from me;
>your mercy and your truth will continually watch over me."*
>~ Psalm 40:11 (NASB)

https://www.hopetoinspireyou.com/2022/04/19/resurrection-appearances/

89

Old City of Jerusalem and Masada

Today we are at the Old City of Jerusalem, which consists of four quarters: the Armenian, Jewish, Muslim, and Christian. Some of the most ancient structures in Jerusalem, the walls, or at least their outlines dating back to biblical times, are in this area.

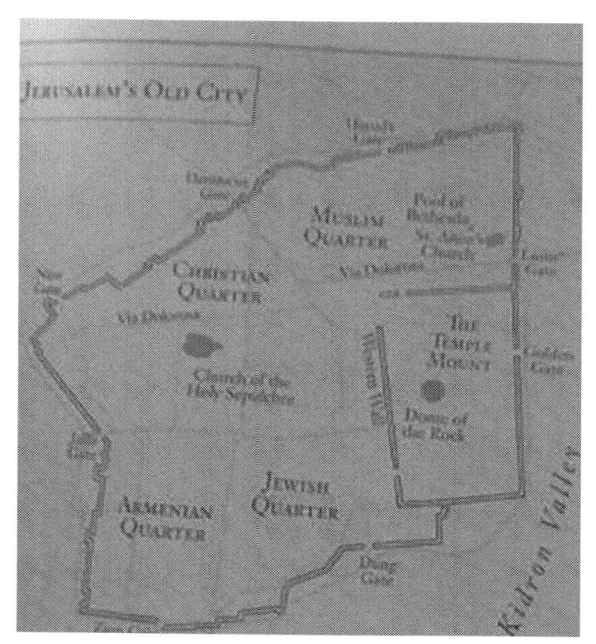

Location of the Four Quarters in the Old City of Jerusalem

The Christian Quarter houses the Holy Sepulchre. The Muslim Quarter is the largest and most populous of the quarters. The Armenian Quarter is the smallest.

The Western Wall is a major landmark in the Jewish Quarter, where we are now. It is the last remnant of the original retaining wall around the Second Temple, which was built over 2000 years ago. It is considered the holiest of places where the Jewish people can pray. Herod the Great had it built. The left section is where the men go to pray, and the ladies go to the right. It was a unique experience to be standing and praying at such a sacred Jewish spot.

The Western Wall

Walking through the four quarters of Old City Jerusalem, I was most impressed to see the acceptance of all people, no matter their religious affiliation. I felt comfortable and at peace walking through all the quarters. I think it is a great lesson for us all about respecting everyone.

"I rejoiced with those who said to me,
'Let us go to the house of the Lord.'
Our feet are standing
in your gates, Jerusalem.
Jerusalem is built like a city
that is closely compacted together.
That is where the tribes go up—
the tribes of the Lord—

> *to praise the name of the Lord*
> *according to the statute given to Israel.*
> *There stand the thrones for judgment,*
> *the thrones of the house of David.*
> *Pray for the peace of Jerusalem:*
> *'May those who love you be secure.*
> *May there be peace within your walls*
> *and security within your citadels.'*
> *For the sake of my family and friends,*
> *I will say, 'Peace be within you.'*
> *For the sake of the house of the Lord our God,*
> *I will seek your prosperity."*
> ~ Psalm 122:1-9

REFLECTION:

Do you make praising the Lord a priority?
How do you share God's peace with others?

As you reflect on our pilgrimage stop today, be encouraged to remember to…

praise the Lord for His goodness.

> *"But Jesus said, 'No, go home to your family,*
> *and tell them everything the Lord has done for you*
> *and how merciful he has been.'"*
> ~ Mark 5:19 (NLT)

https://www.hopetoinspireyou.com/2022/04/26/the-final-pilgrimage-day/

MASADA

Our next stop today is Masada National Park, which offers another spectacular view of part of the southern area of the Judean Desert and overlooks the Dead Sea. We took a cable car to reach the top part, where we were able to see much of the magnificent palace that Herod, King of Judea, had built starting in 35 BC. It was built as both a winter getaway and a haven from enemies. After Herod's death, the ancient Romans overtook Judea in the first century AD, at which time the grounds became a fortress for the Jewish people.

An unexpected opportunity to ride a camel for the first time

Part of King Herod's palace in Masada

The Judean Desert in the background

REFLECTION:

Where is the most picturesque place you have experienced God's beauty? When has God been a fortress for you?

As you reflect on our pilgrimage stop at Masada, be encouraged to remember to…

> see the beauty in God's creation.
> know God is our fortress.

"Turn your ear to me, come quickly to my rescue; be my rock of refuge, a strong fortress to save me. Since you are my rock and my fortress, for the sake of your name lead and guide me."
~ Psalm 31:2-3

https://www.hopetoinspireyou.com/2022/04/26/the-final-pilgrimage-day/

90

Dead Sea and Jaffa

We are off to the Dead Sea in southern Israel, which the Jordan River flows into. It is also known as the Sea of the Arabah, the Eastern Sea, and the Sea of Sodom. At 1,412 feet below sea level, the Dead Sea's shores are the lowest land-based elevation on earth. It has about a 34% salinity rate, compared to the average ocean salinity rate of 3.5%.

I try not to pass up adventures, so I knew I wanted to attempt floating in the Dead Sea, something I normally do not have much success at. Two minutes before getting to the Dead Sea, our tour guide informed us to be aware that we could not swim as one normally does because of the salt content. I am not really a swimmer, so on the one hand, it was a relief. But, I became a little concerned when he mentioned two important things. He emphasized not to swallow any of the water or get it in the eyes because of the bacteria present in the Dead Sea. It was at that time I learned to walk into the water backwards and then pretend to sit. At that point, I would float.

As I made my way down the stairs and through the sand, it became apparent that the Dead Sea was about as muddy and slippery as the Jordan River. I was hoping for the gentleman who helped some of us on different walks would help me get in. This time he said I was on my own. As I approached the water, God provided another person who graciously assisted me by letting me hold both of his hands to get in. I was grateful for the assistance and relieved to be floating. I floated away from the shoreline using my arms and legs, going into deeper water. It suddenly occurred to me that I had not quite processed how I was going to get out of the water. I asked the person who helped me in, who said it was a little hard, but to just push my legs down to stand up. I was still out in deeper water, so I attempted to get to shallower water before trying to lower my legs. I became concerned as I was afraid I would fall forward into the water.

About this time, I began to panic, and my floating turned into my arms and legs flailing, with water splashing into one eye. In my panic, I asked for help, but my helper did not come to my rescue. I was not sure what I was going to do when suddenly, a comforting voice and an arm came from behind me and began pulling me toward the shore. I had no idea who it was, but I was certainly relieved to be taken to shallow water where I opted to just sit for a few minutes. I was grateful to this person, who used to be a lifeguard, and knew the best way to assist a panicking person. It caused me to reflect on the importance of being there for others in their time of need.

A view of the Dead Sea

The Dead Sea is mentioned a few times in Scripture. I believe an important parallel with this passage is how we have abundant life as we continue to grow in faith and trust. Where there was once no life, God will bring to fruition a newness of life.

"He asked me, 'Son of man, do you see this?' Then he led me back to the bank of the river. When I arrived there, I saw a great number of trees on each side of the river. He said to me, 'This water flows toward the eastern region and goes down into the Arabah, where it enters the Dead Sea. When it empties into the sea, the salty water there becomes fresh. Swarms of living creatures will live wherever the river flows. There will be large numbers of fish, because this water flows there and makes the salt water fresh; so where the river flows everything will live. Fishermen will stand along the shore; from En Gedi to En Eglaim there will be places for spreading nets. The fish will be of many kinds— like the fish of the Mediterranean Sea. But the swamps and marshes will not become fresh; they will be left for salt. Fruit trees of all kinds will grow on both banks of the river. Their leaves will not wither, nor will their fruit fail. Every month they will bear fruit, because the water from the sanctuary flows to them. Their fruit will serve for food and their leaves for healing.'"
~ Ezekiel 47:6-12

REFLECTION:

Who has God put in your path to rescue when they need help?
In what way is God calling you to a newness of life?

As you reflect on our pilgrimage stop at the Dead Sea, be encouraged to remember to...

>reach out to those who need a helping hand.

*"No eye pitied you, to do any of these things to you out of compassion for you,
but you were cast out on the open field, for you were abhorred,
on the day that you were born. 'And when I passed by you and
saw you wallowing in your blood,
I said to you in your blood, "Live!"
I said to you in your blood, "Live!"'"*
~ Ezekiel 16:5-6 (ESV)

https://www.hopetoinspireyou.com/2022/04/26/the-final-pilgrimage-day/

JAFFA

Our Holy Land pilgrimage draws to a close with a quick stop to Jaffa, also called Joppa, for a night view of the Mediterranean Sea, which borders Israel on the left. Jaffa is an ancient port city in Israel, located in the southern and oldest part of Tel Aviv-Yafo. The disciple, Peter, stayed at the house of Simon the Tanner in Jaffa. Through the power of the Holy Spirit, Peter performed miracles in Jaffa too.

Our pilgrimage ended with a wonderful feast at St. George's Restaurant before heading to the airport for the 12-hour flight back home, which, you, my reader, have the pleasure of skipping.

The Mediterranean Sea at Jaffa

The probable location of Simon the Tanner's house, mentioned in Acts

"Peter sent them all out of the room; then he got down on his knees and prayed. Turning toward the dead woman, he said, 'Tabitha, get up.' She opened her eyes, and seeing Peter she sat up. He took her by the hand and helped her to her feet. Then he called for the believers, especially the widows, and presented her to them alive. This became known all over Joppa, and many people believed in the Lord. Peter stayed in Joppa for some time with a tanner named Simon."
~ Acts 9:40-43

REFLECTION:

How do you see miracles happening in your life?
How have you seen your faith grow through others' sharing the Holy Spirit's power in their life?

As you reflect on our pilgrimage stop to Jaffa, be encouraged to remember to…

share the Holy Spirit's power working in your life.

"Now as he approached the gate of the city, a dead man was being carried out, the only son of his mother, and she was a widow; and a sizeable crowd from the city was with her. When the Lord saw her, he felt compassion for her and said to her, 'Do not go on weeping.' And he came up and touched the coffin; and the bearers came to a halt. And he said, 'Young man, I say to you, arise!' And the dead man sat up and began to speak. And Jesus gave him back to his mother."
~ Luke 7:12-15 (NASB)

https://www.hopetoinspireyou.com/2022/04/26/the-final-pilgrimage-day/

FAREWELL TO THE HOLY LAND PILGRIMAGE

My dear reader, as we have pilgrimaged together the last several days, I hope you experienced the fifth gospel and met Jesus more intimately. I leave you with this quote that I hope is a reality in your life as a result of your walk in Jesus' footsteps in the Holy Land.

> *"My beloved, there are many testimonies of Christ. The first testimonies are God the Father, the Holy Spirit, the archangels, the Theotokos, the apostles, the winds silenced at Christ's command, the loaves multiplied to feed thousands, the clothes for his burial. But, here you have before you many witnesses. The blessed place of the manger bears witness. The Jordan River bears witness. The Sea of Tiberius bears witness. Gethsemane bears witness. The Mount of Olives bears witness. Most holy Golgotha bears witness. Others only hear, but we both see and touch."*
> ~ St. Cyril of Jerusalem circa A.D. 360

May Jesus continue to reveal Himself to you through the Scriptures and in your life. Thanks for journeying on this pilgrimage. God bless.

https://www.hopetoinspireyou.com/2022/04/26/the-final-pilgrimage-day/

CONCLUSION

As you have journeyed through these 90 devotions, I hope seeing the compassion of God, our Father, Jesus, and the Holy Spirit have illuminated your way. God is always showing His love and compassion for all His children, even when we don't realize it. My prayer is that you will see more of the many ways God lavishes His compassion and love in your life.

I encourage you to keep seeking God, keep looking up to Him, and keep living in His love and compassion. God's compassion is found everywhere— in people, in Scripture, in activities, and in the Holy Land.

I leave you with the poem on the following page that I hope encourages you to see God in everything. May you experience God's love, peace, joy, and compassion in both the good and bad. He is always with us. God bless.

"The fruit of love is service, which is compassion in action."
~ Mother Teresa

"The Lord is merciful and compassionate,
slow to get angry and filled with unfailing love.
The Lord is good to everyone.
He showers compassion on all his creation."
~ Psalm 145:8-9 (NLT)

SEE GOD IN EVERYTHING[4]

"Give me a new idea," I said,
While musing on a sleepless bed;
"A new idea that'll bring to earth
A balm for souls of priceless worth;
That'll give men thoughts of things above,
And teach them how to serve and love,
That'll banish every selfish thought,
And rid men of the sins they've fought."

The new thought came, just how, I'll tell:
'Twas when on bended knee I fell,
And sought from HIM who knows full well
The way our sorrow to expel.
SEE GOD IN ALL THINGS, great and small,
And give HIM praise whate'er befall,
In life or death, in pain or woe,
See God, and overcome thy foe.
I saw HIM in the morning light,
HE made the day shine clear and bright;
I saw HIM in the noontide hour,
And gained from HIM refreshing shower.
At eventide, when worn and sad,
HE gave me help, and made me glad.
At midnight, when on tossing bed
My weary soul to sleep HE led.

*I saw HIM when great losses came,
And found HE loved me just the same.
When heavy loads I had to bear,
I found HE lightened every care.
By sickness, sorrow, sore distress,
HE calmed my mind and gave me rest.
HE'S filled my heart with gladsome praise
Since I gave HIM the upward gaze.
'Twas new to me, yet old to some,
This thought that to me has become
A revelation of the way
We all should live throughout the day;
For as each day unfolds its light,
We'll walk by faith and not by sight.
Life will, indeed, a blessing bring,
If we SEE GOD IN EVERYTHING."*
--A. E. Finn

ABOUT THE AUTHOR

In front of the Mount of Temptation

Christine Fisher is a simple, ordinary gal, a child of God, a lover of Jesus, a daughter, wife, and mother. She models her life after the ministry of Jesus Christ, serving and encouraging the lonely, the homeless, and the hurting. Through writing, Christine shares God's presence, goodness, and grace through the ordinary things in life. She enjoys spending quiet time in nature worshiping the Creator. Christine and her husband, Mark, live in upstate New York.

Publish his glorious deeds among the nations.
Tell everyone about the amazing things he does.
~ 1 Chronicles 16:24 (NLT)

NOTES

1. Lyrics.com, STANDS4 LLC, 2022. "Be Still Lyrics." Accessed October 4, 2022. https://www.lyrics.com/lyric/25210320/The+Fray/Be+Still.
2. Benigni, Roberto. 1997. Life Is Beautiful. United States: Miramax.
3. Lyrics.com, STANDS4 LLC, 2022. "Day By Day [From Godspell] Lyrics." Accessed September 14, 2022. https://www.lyrics.com/lyric/19562273/Godspell/Day+By+Day+%5BFrom+Godspell%5D.
4. Cowman, Mrs. Charles E. Streams in the Desert. Grand Rapids: Zondervan, 1997.

Made in the USA
Columbia, SC
18 February 2023